PRINT'S BEST LETTERHEADS & BUSINESS CARDS

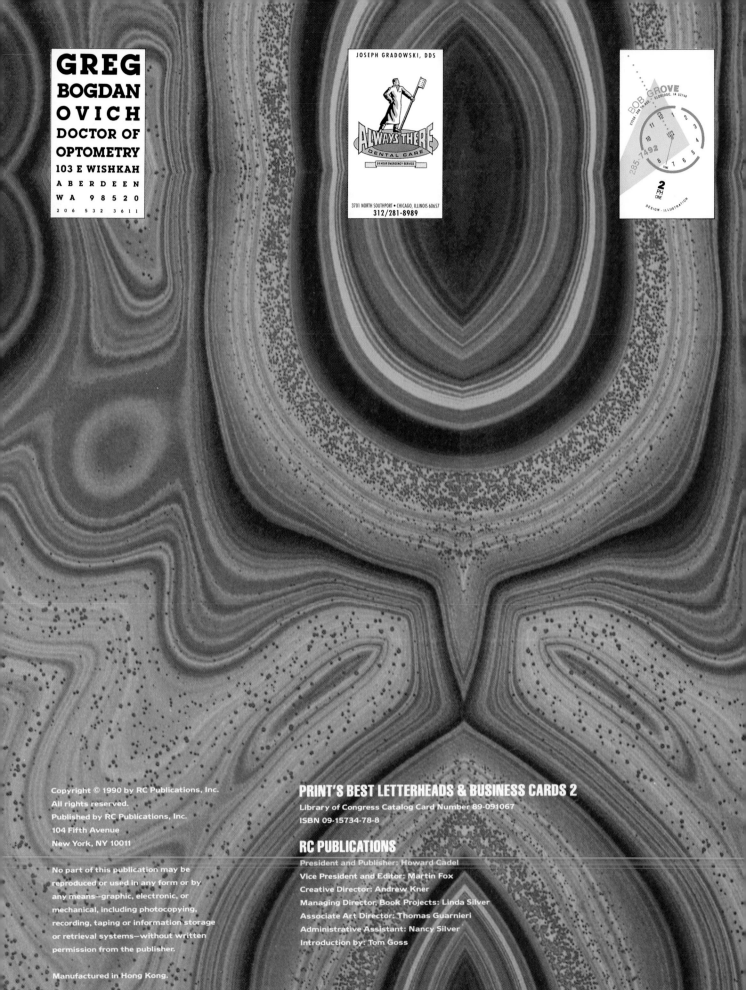

GREG BOGDAN OVICH
DOCTOR OF OPTOMETRY
103 E WISHKAH
ABERDEEN
WA 98520
206 532 3611

JOSEPH GRADOWSKI, DDS

ALWAYS THERE
DENTAL CARE

24 HOUR EMERGENCY SERVICE

3701 NORTH SOUTHPORT • CHICAGO, ILLINOIS 60657
312/281-8989

BOB GROVE

285-7492

2
PH
ONE

DESIGN · ILLUSTRATION

PRINT'S BEST LETTERHEADS & BUSINESS CARDS 2
Library of Congress Catalog Card Number 89-091067
ISBN 09-15734-78-8

RC PUBLICATIONS
President and Publisher: Howard Cadel
Vice President and Editor: Martin Fox
Creative Director: Andrew Kner
Managing Director, Book Projects: Linda Silver
Associate Art Director: Thomas Guarnieri
Administrative Assistant: Nancy Silver
Introduction by: Tom Goss

g.russ
gary russ
photographer

906 East 5th St
Austin TX 78702
(512) 478-4478

I'm John Kneapler, the one on the left.
Graphic/Corporate Design 48 West 21st (2nd Fl)
New York, New York 10010 (212) 463-9774

SEINIGER

TONY SEINIGER
President

Seiniger Advertising, Inc.
8201 West Third Street
Los Angeles, CA 90048-4375
213.653.8665

2

Print's Best
LETTERHEADS &
BUSINESS CARDS
WINNING DESIGNS FROM PRINT MAGAZINE'S NATIONAL COMPETITION

Edited by
LINDA SILVER

Art Directed by
ANDREW KNER

Designed by
THOMAS GUARNIERI

Published by
RC PUBLICATIONS, INC.
NEW YORK, NY

What is good letterhead design? Readers seeking a single, unequivocal answer in this introduction will not find it, but they will find a great many answers by example in the pages that follow. Gathered here are 133 letterheads, business cards, and stationery systems notable enough to have been selected for recent editions of PRINT's Regional Design Annual, itself a product of a competition judged by PRINT's editors and art director.

The purpose of the Regional Design Annual has always been to publish as much of the good work being done around the country as possible, and its popularity attests to its success in that regard. But when so much work is shown in a single volume, the reader isn't always able to fully appreciate certain design projects. In the case of stationery programs, this often means that a single example is chosen to represent the entire system. It is the purpose of the PRINT's Best books to provide this work with a second, more complete showing.

Like the Regional Annual, the PRINT's Best books do not show a bias in favor of any particular design style or esthetic, for that would inevitably exclude a great deal of very fine work, and in the final analysis, would not really represent the breadth of design activity in the U.S. For as PRINT's art director, Andrew Kner, observes, "No style ever dies in American design. There's always someone who comes along and uses it in a way that makes it fresh again." As a result, the following pages contain letterheads in a wide range of styles: from Swiss formalism, to Post-modern, to handcrafted folk art approaches. The criteria that unites these programs are that they are among the best examples of their particular styles and "work" superbly as letterheads.

Letterheads and stationery systems are, next to a logo or symbol, probably the most basic element in any graphic communication system, often being the first graphic communication a potential client sees. And though this collection contains little that might be considered a breakthrough in letterhead or stationery design, it does indicate that a trend cited in the previous edition of this book is gaining in strength: the use of letterheads and other items of stationery as

CONTENTS

INTRODUCTION . . . . **PAGES 4,5**

STATIONERY SYSTEMS . . . . . **PAGES 6-173**

INDEX . . . . **PAGES 174-176**

aggressive promotion pieces and not simply as pieces of paper identifying the sender of the correspondence. This is especially true of letterheads for individuals—they are most pointedly and assertively projecting an individual personality. This assertiveness can take many forms, ranging from elaborate, "lapel-grabbing" production techniques, such as die cuts, embossing, watermarks, and multi-color printing, to humor and on to a variety of deliberately quirky approaches. Not surprisingly, it is individuals "in the business"—designers, illustrators, and photographers—who take this practice to the extreme. The most amusingly blatant examples of using a stationery system as a self-promotion vehicle are those where the individual goes beyond the standard name, address, and telephone number to add little messages. (One such message, appearing on a designer's invoicing form, apologetically explains that billing the customer was her brother-in-law's idea.) Others put their own picture on the letterhead, while some photographers have taken the unorthodox step of using illustrated imagery that though it doesn't relate directly to photography, does lead the viewer to the concept by means of a pun or other humorous association.

Some of the programs shown here consist of a single piece, either because that's all that was produced or all that was available from a discontinued program. Others range from basic letterhead and envelope to full-blown systems that include invoices, memos, and other business forms. The variety of businesses, individuals, styles, and approaches to stationery systems argues against forcing the work in this volume into arbitrary categories. Instead, it is presented with an eye toward comparing and contrasting themes, styles, and production techniques. In some cases, for example, a series of programs using a similar image may be grouped together to show how the same idea can have many different and original applications. Other pages display the astonishing variety of approaches designers can take to something as simple as a business card. This method of presentation, we feel, enhances this book's value as both a catalog of outstanding letterhead designs and as an important reference source for designers. —*Tom Goss*

S E I N I G E R

TONY SEINIGER
President

Seiniger Advertising, Inc.
8201 West Third Street
Los Angeles, CA 90048-4375
213 . 653 . 8665

S E I N I G E R

Seiniger Advertising, Inc.
8201 West Third Street
Los Angeles, CA 90048-4375
213 . 653 . 8665 Fax 213 . 653 . 9150

Seiniger Advertising

Seiniger Advertising, Inc.
8201 West Third Street
Los Angeles, CA 90048-4375

DESIGN FIRM: Scott W.

Miller Design Group,

Los Angeles, California

DESIGNER: Scott W.

Miller

Seiniger Advertising, Inc.

8201 West Third Street Los Angeles, CA 90048-4375   213 . 653 . 8665

The Children's Doctors

St. Joseph Medical Place I • 1315 Calhoun, Suite 1403 • Houston, Texas 77002 • 713-650-0650

Stephen E. Whitney, M.D., F.A.A.P.
Diane H. Freeman, M.D.

DESIGN FIRM: Ramsden Design, Houston, Texas

DESIGNER: Rosalie Ramsden

ILLUSTRATOR: Bill Kantz

COPYWRITER: Steve Barnhill

The Children's Doctors

Health Care for Young People

Se Habla Espanol.

The Children's Doctors • St. Joseph Medical Place I
1315 Calhoun, Suite 1403 • Houston, Texas 77002
713-650-0650

Rx The Kid's Club

The Children's Doctors

St. Joseph Medical Place I
1315 Calhoun, Suite 1403 • Houston, Texas 77002 • 713-650-0650

The Children's Doctors
St. Joseph Medical Place I
1315 Calhoun, Suite 1403 • Houston, Texas 77002

JOSEPH GRADOWSKI, DDS

3701 NORTH SOUTHPORT • CHICAGO, ILLINOIS 60657
312/281-8989

2200 NORTH HALSTED
CHICAGO, IL 60614

SCOTT STIFFLE, DDS. · DAVID FIORE, DDS.
2200 NORTH HALSTED · CHICAGO, ILLINOIS 60614 · 312/348-0565

DESIGN FIRM: Michael
Carr Design, Chicago,
Illinois

**DESIGNER/
ILLUSTRATOR:** Michael
Carr

**SIGNAGE
FABRICATORS:** Raul
Campoverde, Rich
Sprankle

Always There Dental Care

TAKE A STAND FOR YOUR SMILE

IT'S TIME AGAIN FOR YOUR REGULAR DENTAL EXAMINATION.

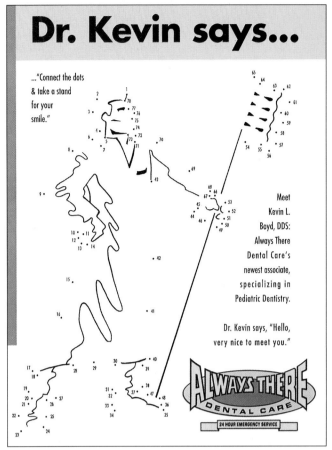

Dr. Kevin says...

..."Connect the dots & take a stand for your smile."

Meet Kevin L. Boyd, DDS: Always There Dental Care's newest associate, specializing in Pediatric Dentistry.

Dr. Kevin says, "Hello, very nice to meet you."

ALWAYS THERE DENTAL CARE
24 HOUR EMERGENCY SERVICE

ALWAYS THERE DENTAL CARE
24 HOUR EMERGENCY SERVICE

11

Mel Fagan Swing Co.

DESIGN FIRM: Borders,

Perrin & Norrander,

Portland, Oregon

DESIGNER/

ILLUSTRATOR: Athena

Thompson

Nancy Steinman Advertising Design

DESIGN FIRM: Nancy

Steinman Advertising

Design, Reseda,

California

DESIGNER: Nancy

Steinman

DESIGN FIRM: Studio

Bustamante, San Diego,

California

DESIGNER/

ILLUSTRATOR: Gerald

Bustamante

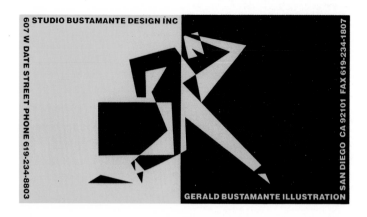

Gerald Bustamante

DESIGNER: Karen

Stiegler Lupton,

Lynchburg, Virginia

COPYWRITER: Vivian

Alford

Vivian Alford (Copywriter)

JOHN S. DYKES ILLUSTRATION 203-222-8150

FRANK METZ
SIMON & SCHUSTER
SUB OF GULF & WESTERN
1230 AVE OF THE AMERICAS
NEW YORK   NY 10020

URGENT

DESIGNER/

ILLUSTRATOR: John S.

Dykes, Westport,

Connecticut

John S. Dykes

JOHN S. DYKES
203-222-8150

Van Horn Photography
2020 N. Main Street #224
Los Angeles, California 90031
213/222-2175

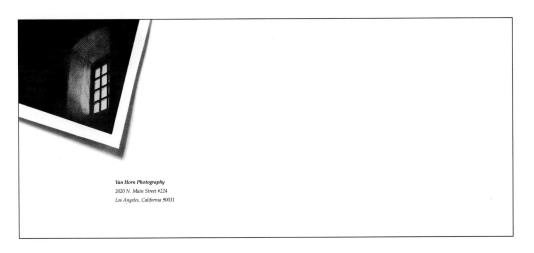

Van Horn Photography
2020 N. Main Street #224
Los Angeles, California 90031

DESIGN FIRM: Hershey
Associates, Los Angeles,
California
ART DIRECTOR:
R. Christine Hershey
DESIGNER: Nick McNeil

Van Horn Photography
2020 N. Main Street #224
Los Angeles, California 90031
213/222-2175

Susan Van Horn

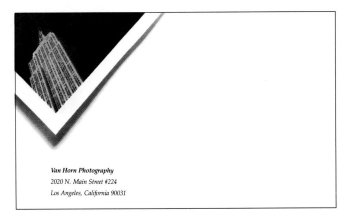

Van Horn Photography
2020 N. Main Street #224
Los Angeles, California 90031

DESIGN FIRM: Brenda Behr Advertising Design, Minneapolis, Minnesota
DESIGNER: Brenda Behr
PHOTOGRAPHER: Sue Mills
COPYWRITER: Leslie Carlson Ritchie

Leslie Carlson Ritchie (Advertising Writer/Producer)

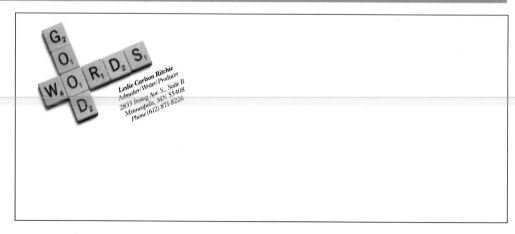

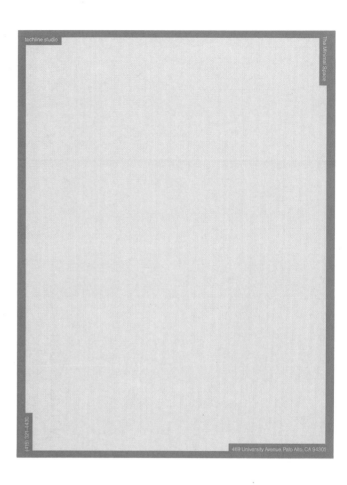

DESIGN FIRM: Sam

Smidt, Inc., Palo Alto,

California

DESIGNER: Sam Smidt

Diversified Packaging

DESIGN FIRM: Weeks & Associates, Perrysburg, Ohio

DESIGNER: Dan Weeks

Diversified Packaging Company

Unlimited Options in Packaging

1178 Bernath Parkway
Toledo, Ohio
43615-6742
419/865-1747
Fax #:
419/865-3721

Diversified Packaging Company

1178 Bernath Parkway
Toledo, Ohio
43615-6742

DESIGN FIRM: McKinlay and Partners, Farmington, Connecticut
CREATIVE DIRECTOR: Lee A. Hill
DESIGNER: David Martino

stĕv pitt

2549 cherry, kcmo, 64108

2549 cherry, kcmo, 64108   816-471-3673

DESIGN FIRM: Jan Tracy

Design, Kansas City,

Missouri

ART DIRECTOR/

DESIGNER/

ILLUSTRATOR: Jan Tracy

Stĕv Pitt (Mock-Ups & Prototypes)

stĕv pitt

2549 cherry, kcmo, 64108   816-471-3673

2, 3, 4 – d mockups & prototypes

816-471-3673

stĕv pitt

Picks:

Multi-restaurant
housing systems

Three Lincoln Centre
5430 LBJ Freeway
Suite 1600
Dallas, Texas 75240
214 387 1250
Telefax 214 934 0042

DESIGN FIRM: Eisenberg,

Pannell, St. George,

Dallas, Texas

ART DIRECTORS: Brent

Anderson, Arthur

Eisenberg

DESIGNER/

ILLUSTRATOR: Brent

Anderson

Picks:

Multi-restaurant
housing systems

Three Lincoln Centre
5430 LBJ Freeway
Suite 1600
Dallas, Texas 75240

Pick's Multi-Restaurant Housing Systems

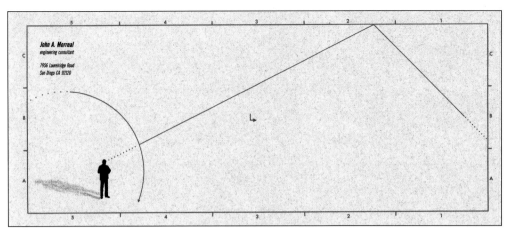

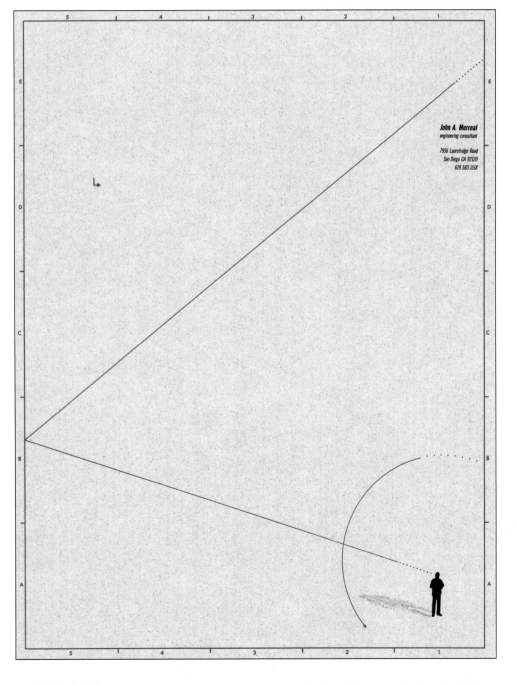

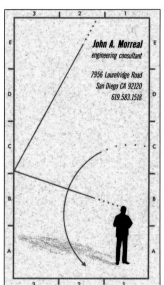

DESIGN FIRM: Morreal

Graphic Design,

San Diego, California

DESIGNER: Mary Lou

Morreal

Twigs, Inc.
381 Bleeker Street
New York, New York 10014

Twigs, Inc.
381 Bleeker Street
New York, New York 10014

DESIGN FIRM: Lewin

Design Associates,

New York, New York

DESIGNER: Cheryl Lewin

Twigs, Inc. (Florist)

Twigs, Inc.   381 Bleeker Street   New York, New York 10014   212 620 8188   ·   3 World Financial Center   New York, New York 10281   212 385 2660

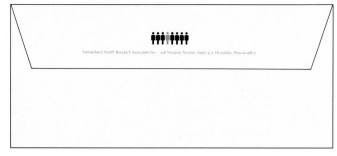

Barbara L. Sunderland
President

Sunderland Smith, Research Associates Inc.
928 Nuuanu Avenue, Suite 403
Honolulu, Hawaii 96817
Telephone 808 526-3717
Marketing Research/Public Opinion Polling

Sunderland Smith Research Associates (Marketing/Polling)

DESIGN FIRM:

Linschoten & Associates,

Inc., Honolulu, Hawaii

DESIGNER: Bud

Linschoten

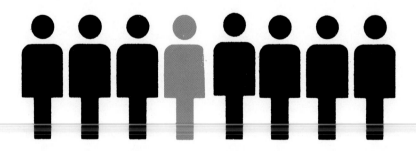

DESIGN FIRM:

Stonecreek Designs,

South Salem, New York

DESIGNER: Carolyn

Bucha

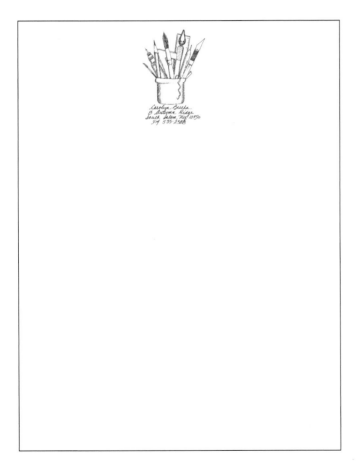

Elements
Of
Style
(201) 670-7551

Interior
Designer,
L. Shamsey

P.O. Box 1145
Ridgewood,
New Jersey
07451

Elements
Of
Style

Interior
Designer,
L. Shamsey

Ridgewood,
New Jersey
(201) 670-7551

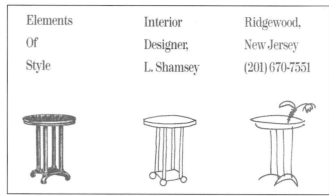

DESIGN FIRM: Ganz

Goldman

DESIGNER/

ILLUSTRATOR: Bobbie

Friedman, Cranston,

Rhode Island

COPYWRITER: Bonnie

Ganz

Elements
Of
Style

P.O. Box
1145

Ridgewood,
New Jersey
07451

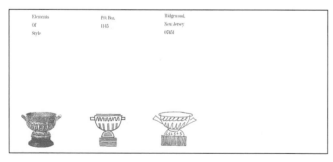

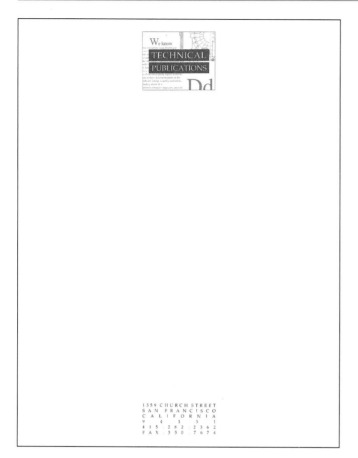

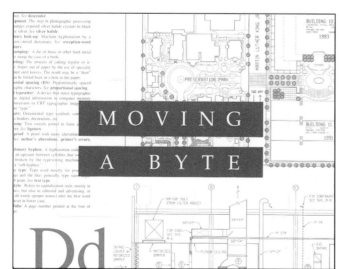

DESIGNER: Patricia

Belichick, San Francisco,

California

CANTEEN CLOTHING, INC.
9615 BRIGHTON WAY
BEVERLY HILLS, CA 90210
213 858-3925
213 276-8092 FAX

DESIGN FIRM: Victoria Miller Design, Los Angeles, California

DESIGNER: Victoria Miller

CLIENT: Camp Beverly Hills

CANTEEN CLOTHING, INC.
9615 BRIGHTON WAY
BEVERLY HILLS, CA 90210

JEFFREY A. STEIN
PRESIDENT

CANTEEN CLOTHING, INC.
9615 BRIGHTON WAY
BEVERLY HILLS, CA 90210
213 858-3925
213 276-8092 FAX

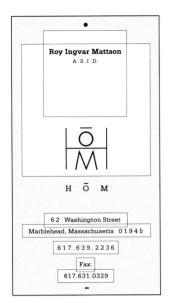

Roy Ingvar Mattson
A.S.I.D.

H Ō M

62 Washington Street
Marblehead, Massachusetts 01945

617.639.2236

Fax:
617.631.0329

H Ō M

62 Washington Street
Marblehead, Massachusetts 01945

617.639.2236

Fax:
617.631.0329

DESIGN FIRM: Skolos/

Wedell, Inc., Charlestown,

Massachusetts

ART DIRECTOR: Nancy

Skolos

DESIGNER: Mark

Sylvester

H Ō M

HōM (Interior Design)

DESIGN FIRM: Grand Pré
and Whaley, Ltd., St.
Paul, Minnesota
DESIGNER/
ILLUSTRATOR: Kevin
Whaley
CLIENT: Chargo Printing/
The Art Department

1336 ENERGY PARK DRIVE
SAINT PAUL, MN 55108
TELEPHONE: 612 642 1204

1336 ENERGY PARK DRIVE · SAINT PAUL, MN 55108 · TELEPHONE: 612 642 1204

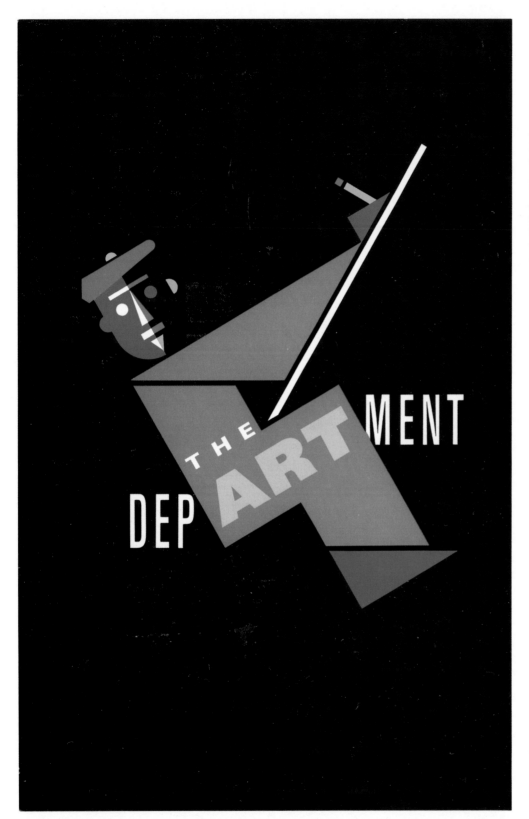

TERI WILSON

1336 ENERGY PARK DRIVE

SAINT PAUL, MN 55108

TELEPHONE: 612 642 1204

The Art Department (Design/Illustration/Pagination Typesetting/Keylining)

DESIGN FIRM: Michael

Stanard, Inc., Evanston,

Illinois

ART DIRECTOR/

DESIGNER: Marcos

Chavez

Wesley James Bender Photography

DESIGN FIRM: Maclean

Eckert Communications,

Chicago, Illinois

ART DIRECTOR: Lisa

Eckert

CALLIGRAPHER: Robert

Horn

TYPOGRAPHER:

Deborah Maclean

PRINTER: Deforest

Printing

PAT URBAN

PHOTO
STYLIST

100
Southern Parkway
Rochester
New York
14618
716 442 3384

PAT URBAN

PHOTO
STYLIST

100

Southern Parkway

Rochester

New York

14618

716 442 3384

DESIGN FIRM: Dunn and

Rice Design, Rochester,

New York

DESIGNER: John Dunn

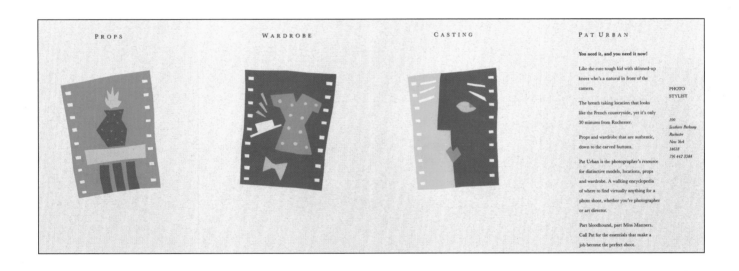

PROPS   WARDROBE   CASTING   PAT URBAN

You need it, and you need it now!

Like the cute tough kid with skinned-up
knees who's a natural in front of the
camera.

The breath taking location that looks
like the French countryside, yet it's only
30 minutes from Rochester.

Props and wardrobe that are authentic,
down to the carved buttons.

Pat Urban is the photographer's resource
for distinctive models, locations, props
and wardrobe. A walking encyclopedia
of where to find virtually anything for a
photo shoot, whether you're photographer
or art director.

Part bloodhound, part Miss Manners.
Call Pat for the essentials that make a
job become the perfect shoot.

PHOTO
STYLIST

100
Southern Parkway
Rochester
New York
14618
716 442 3384

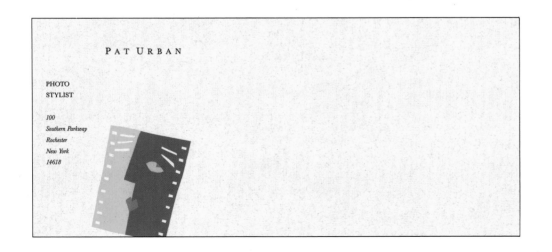

PAT URBAN

PHOTO
STYLIST

100
Southern Parkway
Rochester
New York
14618

1025 Ocean Avenue #205 ● Santa Monica, CA 90403 ● 213-458-2633, FAX-213-394-4559

1025 Ocean Avenue #205 ● Santa Monica, CA 90403

Lauren Brenner-Katz Advertising (Direct-Response)

213-458-2633
FAX-213-394-4559

Lauren Brenner-Katz
Direct Response Advertising
1025 Ocean Avenue #205
Santa Monica, CA 90403

DESIGN FIRM: Lauren

Brenner-Katz

Advertising, Santa

Monica, California

DESIGNER: Darrin

Brenner

Post Office Box 897
Kailua, Hawaii 96734

Phone 808·261·6075
Fax 808·2636·019

Think Positive!

Think Positive!

DESIGN FIRM: Beatson Vermeer Design, Honolulu, Hawaii
DESIGNER: Dale Vermeer
ILLUSTRATORS: Dan Garrett, Christine Harris, Wally Amos

Wally Amos (Watermelon Memorabilia Collector)

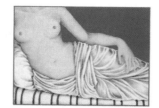

H E A L T H F A S T
for
women

(512) 473-8566
2905 SAN GABRIEL
SUITE 309
AUSTIN, TEXAS
78703

DR. DONNA HURLEY
DR. MARGARET THOMPSON
MEDICAL DIRECTORS

A medically supervised weight-loss program for women.

DESIGN FIRM: Caesar Studio, Austin, Texas

DESIGNER: Delane Caesar

ILLUSTRATOR: Aletha Reppel

DESIGN FIRM: Knoth &

Meads, San Diego,

California

DESIGNER: José Serrano

ILLUSTRATOR: Tracy

Sabin

Robert F. Hernandez
Investigator
Post Office Box 9910
San Diego, CA 92109
Phone 619 488-4044

Post Office Box 9910
San Diego, CA 92109
Phone 619 488-4044

916/641-5707

SACRAMENTO, CALIFORNIA 95834

717 W. DEL PASO ROAD

COFFEE EQUIPMENT
REPAIR SPECIALISTS

TOM WEBORG

Brew Tech (Coffee Equipment Repair)

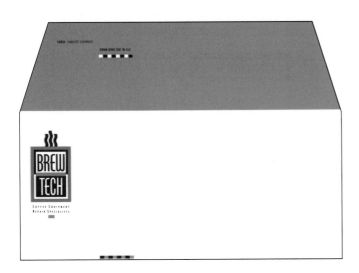

DESIGN FIRM: The Dunlavey Studio, Sacramento, California

ART DIRECTOR: Michael Dunlavey

DESIGNER: Heidi Tomlinson

ART DIRECTOR/

DESIGNER: Arnold

Remer, Toledo, Ohio

**RC ZIMMERMAN
AND ASSOCIATES**
3126 W. SYLVANIA AVE.
TOLEDO, OHIO 43613

**STRATEGIC TARGET
MARKETING**

TO

At RC Zimmerman and
Associates, we mix
strategic thinking with
superior marketing skills
to create results-oriented
promotions and programs
for quality-conscious
clients.

ON TIME

At RC Zimmerman and
Associates, we tell time by
two clocks: yours, and the
marketplace's. That means we
deliver projects on time, every
time—and we build timeliness
and urgency into every sales
message we create. Management has hands-on involvement
in every assignment—to ensure
efficiency and accuracy every
step of the way, from concept
to finished project.

ON TARGET

Today's constantly shrinking
profit margins are expanding
the value of our services. As
clients scrutinize expenditures,
they quickly see the value of
strategic target marketing.
That's why RC Zimmerman
and Associates never waste
time or money on a shotgun
approach to marketing
challenges. We aim right at
the bull's-eye—with powerful
ammunition. To find out how
consistently we hit the mark,
just ask our clients.

ON BUDGET

You can't put a price on
creativity—but you can put
budgetary restraints on RC
Zimmerman and Associates
and expect us to respect them.
Decades of experience have
taught us how to achieve max-
imum efficiency from every
dollar. We're street smart, with
a full understanding of the value
of not just a dollar, but a penny
as well. For us, practical, afford-
able solutions are all in a day's
work. And for our clients, low-
trauma bills are one of the joys
of doing business with us.

LAND PLANNING AND DESIGN

JAMES TAYLOR AND ASSOCIATES
415 E. MICHELTORENA, SUITE C
SANTA BARBARA, CALIF., 93101
8 0 5 - 9 6 5 - 8 3 8 7

DESIGN FIRM: Rick King

Design, Stockton,

California

DESIGNER: Rick King

James Taylor & Associates (Land Planning & Design)

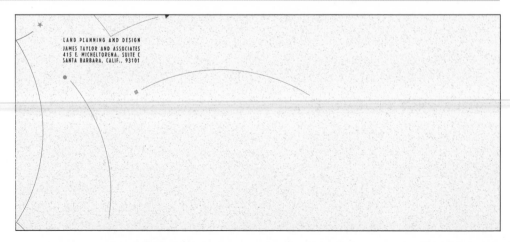

LAND PLANNING AND DESIGN
JAMES TAYLOR AND ASSOCIATES
415 E. MICHELTORENA, SUITE C
SANTA BARBARA, CALIF., 93101

David Butler Illustration

DESIGN FIRM: River City

Studio, Kansas City,

Missouri

ART DIRECTOR/

DESIGNER: David Butler

7901-168th Avenue Northeast, Suite 103, Redmond, Washington 98052

7901 168th Ave. N.E., Suite 103, Redmond, WA 98052

SEE THE BEST BIKE RACERS IN THE NATION.

The 1989 Washington Mutual
U.S. Track Cycling Championships
July 25-29, 1989
Marymoor Velodrome
Redmond, Washington

DESIGN FIRM: Evans/

Spangler Design, Seattle,

Washington

ART DIRECTOR: Kathryn

Spangler

DESIGNER: Ross Hogin

ILLUSTRATOR: Meredith

Yasui

CALLIGRAPHER: Glenn

Yoshiyama

SEE THE BEST BIKE
RACERS IN THE NATION.

The Event. The 1989 Washington Mutual U.S. Track
Cycling Championships, July 25-29, 1989.
Marymoor Velodrome — Redmond, Washington.

The Competitors. Olympic Gold Medalists Mark Gorski
and Steve Hegg. Olympic Silver Medalists Rebecca Twigg
and Leonard Nitz. Pan Am Games champion Ken Carpenter.
World Championship Medalists Connie Young, Janie Eickoff,
and Peggy Maass. And top national caliber riders from the
Pacific Northwest, like Ron Storer and Renee Duprel.

The Races. Matched Sprints, Individual Pursuits,
Kilometer Time Trials, Tandem Sprints, Team Pursuits,
Points Races.

The Dates And Times. 10:00 a.m. Sessions: July 25,
27, 28 (Tuesday, Thursday, Friday). 7:00 p.m. Sessions:
Daily, July 25-29 (Tuesday-Saturday).

The Number. 822-RIDE.

Don't miss the biggest cycling event in Washington this
year. For tickets — or more information — call today!

Johanna B. Hantel
GRAPHIC DESIGN
& ILLUSTRATION
437 E. Belvidere St. F-8
Nazareth, Penna. 18064
215 759 2025
201 635 5264

JOHANNA
BANANA
FE...FI...FOFANA...
JOHANNA

Johanna B. Hantel

DESIGNER/

ILLUSTRATOR: Johanna

B. Hantel, Nazareth,

Pennsylvania

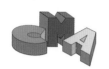

THE CHILDREN'S MUSEUM OF ATLANTA
P.O. BOX 7684, ATLANTA, GA 30357
(404) 875-KIDS

W E   A R E   T H E   F U T U R E

THE CHILDREN'S MUSEUM OF ATLANTA
P. O. BOX 7684, ATLANTA, GA 30357
(404) 875-KIDS

DR. JUNE SCHNEIDER

DESIGN FIRM: Trousdell

Design, Inc., Atlanta,

Georgia

DESIGNER: Don

Trousdell

POST

OFFICE

BOX

133

DES MOINES

IOWA

50301

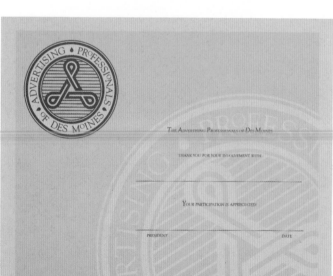

The Advertising Professionals of Des Moines

THANK YOU FOR YOUR INVOLVEMENT WITH

_____

Your Participation is Appreciated

_____   _____
PRESIDENT   DATE

DESIGN FIRM: Sayles

Graphic Design,

Des Moines, Iowa

ART DIRECTOR: John

Sayles

POST

OFFICE

BOX

133

DES MOINES

IOWA

50301

POST

OFFICE

BOX

133

DES MOINES

IOWA

50301

DESIGN FIRM: Toto

Images, New York, New

York

ART DIRECTOR: Andy

Lun

DESIGNERS: Andy Lun,

Jeffrey Huang

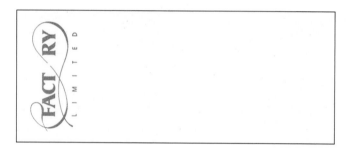

The Factory Limited (Fashion)

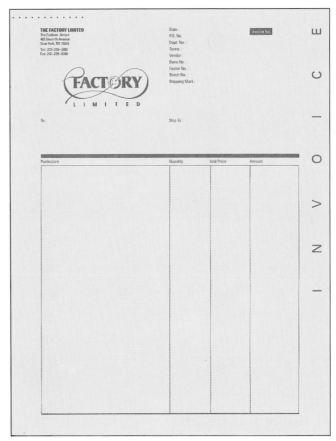

Office & Commissary ♦ 935 S. Wolfe St. ♦ Baltimore MD 21231 ♦ 301.563.4300

The Food Company (Catering)

DESIGN FIRM: Graffito, Inc., Baltimore, Maryland

ART DIRECTOR: Tim Thompson

DESIGNER/ ILLUSTRATOR: Joe Parisi

Bread Selections

Rye	Sunflower Seed	
Marble Rye	Sno-cap White	
Whole Wheat	Pita Pockets	
Sourdough		no charge
Bagels		Ⓐ
Crusty Baguette/Grinder		Ⓑ
Croissant		Ⓒ

Extras

avocado slices (seasonal)	Guacamole (seasonal)	market
Hot peppers Sweet pepperoncini Pesto mayonnaise		Ⓐ
Coleslaw Sprouts		Ⓐ
Hummus		Ⓐ
Bacon		Ⓐ

Dressings

Deli mustard	Russian dressing	
Honey mustard	Italian vinaigrette	
Horseradish	American mayonnaise	no charge

BEVERAGES

Coke	Diet Coke	Sprite	Ⓐ

Specialty Drinks and Juices

iced tea or coffee		Ⓐ
assorted Soho		Ⓐ
orange juice		Ⓐ
grapefruit juice	Dr. Brown's Creme	Ⓐ
cranberry juice	Dr. Brown's Black Cherry	Ⓐ
San Pelligrino	Perrier plain/lemon	Ⓐ
lemonade (seasonal)		Ⓐ

BOX LUNCHES
Priced per box.

Standard Assorted deli sandwiches, potato salad/cole slaw, chips, brownie, fruit salad Ⓑ⁷⁵

Oriental 3 marinated oriental chicken and vegetable skewers with sesame-ginger sauce, sesame noodles with broccoli, pita rounds with oriental sesame-scallion butter, fruit salad, almond cookies/fortune cookies Ⓑ⁷⁵

Southwestern Stuffed zucchini boats with jalapeno chicken salad, cornbread or sourdough with honey butter, picnic pasta – tri color pasta with vegetables tossed in an herbed vinaigrette, fruit, brownie or pecan shortbread Ⓐ⁷⁵

Vegetarian Pita stuffed with marinated vegetables, avocado (seasonal) and munster cheese, pasta salad with seasonal vegetables tossed in an Italian-parmesan vinaigrette, fruit, cookies Ⓑ⁷⁵

Mediterranean Wedge of cheese, seafood salad, hard french roll/butter, Greek salad, fruit, cookies Ⓑ⁷⁵

Southern Picnic Fried chicken breast (or for special diets - baked), sourdough bread/butter, cole slaw or pasta primavera, fruit, brownie or blondie Ⓐ⁷⁵

Italian Antipasto salad, herbed Italian garlic bread, Caesar salad, fruit, Italian cookies (biscotti) Ⓐ⁹⁵

Sushi-Box Assorted sushi displayed decoratively in a black lacquer box, fresh fruit, almond cookies, coconut bonbons Ⓐ⁶⁵

Suzanne's
Cakes and Pastries

301 West Sixth Street   Medford, Oregon 97501   Telephone: (503) 779-8022

DESIGN FIRM: Ted Bertz Design, Inc., Middletown, Connecticut
ART DIRECTOR: Ted Bertz
DESIGNER/ ILLUSTRATOR: Keri Beaton

Suzanne's Cakes & Pastries

Suzanne's
Cakes and Pastries

TA_G LETTER

THE ALFSTAD BLANK GROUP   485 Fifth Avenue New York, New York 10017   212.687.1784   Fax 212.490.0192

TA_G copy

THE ALFSTAD BLANK GROUP   485 Fifth Avenue New York, New York 10017   212.687.1784   Fax 212.490.0192

The Alfstad Blank Group

TA_G MAIL

THE ALFSTAD BLANK GROUP   485 Fifth Avenue New York, New York 10017

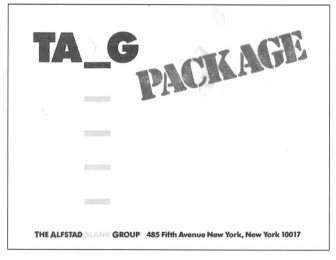

TA_G PACKAGE

THE ALFSTAD BLANK GROUP   485 Fifth Avenue New York, New York 10017

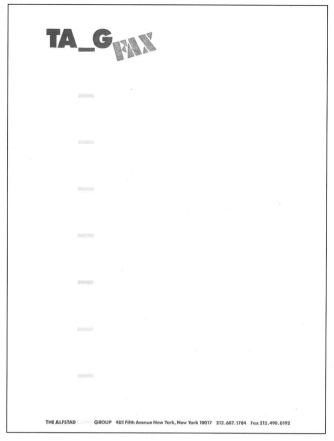

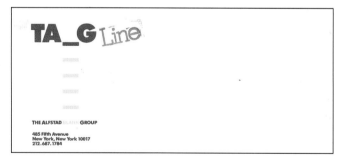

DESIGN FIRM: The

Alfstad Blank Group,

New York, New York

CREATIVE DIRECTORS:

Peter J. Blank, Sam

Alfstad

(Say...)

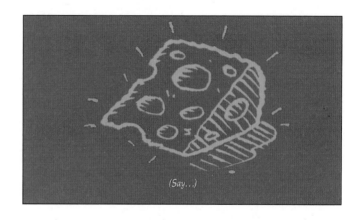

(Say...)

IMBROGNO PHOTOGRAPHY
935 West Chestnut Street Suite 301 Chicago, Illinois 60622
Phone 312.733.3650 Fax 312.733.3569
Gordon Kleber *(Representative)*

Jim Imbrogno *(Big Cheese)*

DESIGN FIRM: Pressley

Jacobs Design, Inc.,

Chicago, Illinois

DESIGNER: William Lee

Johnson

ILLUSTRATOR: Steve

Musgrave

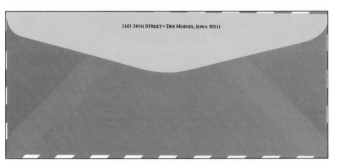

1163 24TH STREET • DES MOINES, IOWA 50311

1163 24TH STREET • DES MOINES, IOWA 50311 • (515) 277-3647 • (515) 277-DOGS

DESIGN FIRM: Sayles

Graphic Design,

Des Moines, Iowa

DESIGNER: John Sayles

ILLUSTRATORS: John

Sayles, Joe Dudak

1163 24TH STREET • DES MOINES, IOWA 50311 • (515) 277-3647 • (515) 277-DOGS

LET CHICAGO DOG AND DELI
EXTINGUISH YOUR HUNGER AND THIRST!

ALARMINGLY GOOD SANDWICHES

Hot Dog	$1.79
(100% Vienna Beef® dog)	
Jumbo Dog	$2.29
(quarter pound top dog)	
Chili Dog	$2.29
Jumbo Chili Dog	$2.79
(top dog with chili)	
Grilled Polish	$2.29
(a rare breed)	
Top Bratwurst	$2.29
Barbecued Beef	$3.29
(blazing with flavor)	
Italian Beef	$3.29
Italian Sausage	$3.29
Combination Italian ..	$3.79
(beef and sausage combo)	
Corned Beef	$2.99
Roast Beef	$2.99
Turkey	$2.79
Salami	$3.29
Tuna Salad	$2.29
Egg Salad	$2.29

"For only $1 extra on any sandwich order,
get fries, and beans or coleslaw. That's a hot deal!

"Chicago Style" includes:
hot or regular mustard, relish, pickle,
tomato, onion, hot peppers,
and celery salt on a poppy seed bun.
(Other "stuff" available — just ask!)

Onion bun: 10¢ extra.
Cheddar, Swiss, Muenster, or hot pepper
cheese on any deli sandwich - add 15¢.

SIDE ORDERS

Coleslaw	$ .79
Baked Beans	$ .79
Fresh Cut Fries	$ .79
Chili	$1.59
Soup	$1.59
Side Salad	$1.79
Salad Rounds	$2.99
(all you can eat salad bar)	

DRINKS

All you can drink	$ .79
Pepsi, Diet Pepsi, Mountain Dew, Slice,	
Dad's® Root Beer, iced tea, or lemonade	
Coffee, tea	$ .69
Milk	$ .59
Beer .... Domestic	$1.50
Import	$2.25

Conveniently located in
"DOG TOWN." Call ahead for
fast takeout service!

Chicago Dog and Deli is the
top dog in catering
call us for your next event.

Typing
(to go)

Grace Hanneman
922-1724
1380 S. Eaton Street
Lakewood, CO 80226

DESIGN FIRM: Penguin

Studio/Press, Denver,

Colorado

DESIGNER: Catherine J.

Ayers

Typing to Go

65

BELKOWITZ HOPKINS PHOTOGRAPHY 408 VINE ST SUITE 2B PHILA PA 19106 215 629.1802 FAX 923.4185

Bel-Hop Studio (Photography)

DESIGN FIRM: Ilene Griff

Design, Philadelphia,

Pennsylvania

DESIGNER: Ilene Griff

ILLUSTRATOR: Murray

Callahan

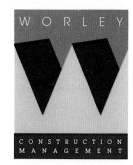

P.O. BOX 33346
SAN DIEGO
CALIFORNIA
9 2 1 0 3

619.238.7307
FAX 619.238.0158

DESIGN FIRM: Tyler Blik

Design, San Diego,

California

ART DIRECTOR: Tyler

Blik

DESIGNERS: Ken Soto,

Anita Frederick

P.O. BOX 33346
SAN DIEGO
CALIFORNIA
9 2 1 0 3

P.O. BOX 33346
SAN DIEGO
CALIFORNIA
9 2 1 0 3

STEVE WORLEY

619.238.7307
FAX 619.238.0158

EASTERDAY

CONSTRUCTION

·AND DESIGN·

317·257·9757

500 RIPPLE RD

INDIANAPOLIS

INDIANA 46208

DESIGN FIRM: Dean

Johnson Design Inc.,

Indianapolis, Indiana

DESIGNER/

ILLUSTRATOR: Bruce

Dean

Easterday Construction and Design

CAMERON D. POPKIN

BUSINESS MANAGEMENT

√   4442 VAN NOORD AVENUE, STUDIO CITY, CA 91604

(818)
990 7139

DESIGN FIRM: Ph.D.,

Santa Monica, California

ART DIRECTORS: Clive

Piercy, Michael Hodgson

DESIGNER: Michael

Hodgson

PRINTER: Blair Graphics

CAMERON D. POPKIN
BUSINESS MANAGEMENT

√   4442 VAN NOORD AVENUE, STUDIO CITY, CA 91604

CAMERON D. POPKIN

BUSINESS MANAGEMENT

4442 VAN NOORD AVENUE
STUDIO CITY, CA 91604

(818)
990 7139

CAMERON D. POPKIN
BUSINESS MANAGEMENT

√   4442 VAN NOORD AVENUE, STUDIO CITY, CA 91604

CAN

Children's AIDS Network
21 Washington Place, New York, NY 10003, (212) 415-6615

Bryan Miskle, Founder, Chairman

CAN

Children's AIDS Network
21 Washington Place, New York, NY 10003

Children's AIDS Network

DESIGN FIRM: The
Pushpin Group, New
York, New York
DESIGNER/
ILLUSTRATOR: Seymour
Chwast

DAVID R. GARNAND A.I.A.
ARCHITECT

777 ROCKAWAY BEACH AVENUE, PACIFICA, CA 94044. 415-359-8856

DESIGN FIRM: Art Kirsch Graphic Design, Palo Alto, California
DESIGNER: Art Kirsch
ILLUSTRATOR: Charlotte Kirsch

DAVID R. GARNAND A.I.A.
ARCHITECT

777 ROCKAWAY BEACH AVE. PACIFICA, CA 94044. 415-359-8856

DESIGN FIRM: Design
Team One, Inc.,
Cincinnati, Ohio
DESIGNER: Dan Bittman
ILLUSTRATOR: Sara
Gaddis

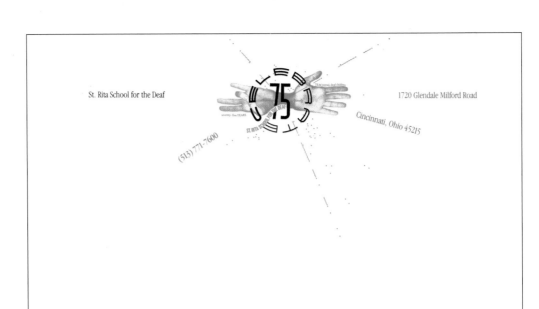

St. Rita School for the Deaf

1720 Glendale Milford Road

Cincinnati, Ohio 45215

(513) 771-7600

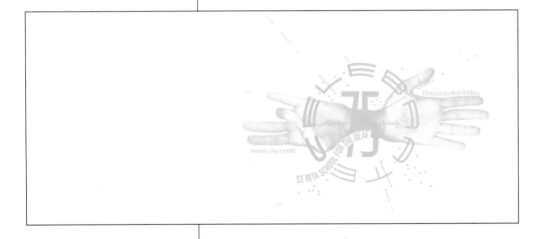

St. Rita School for the Deaf (75th Anniversary)

St. Rita School for the Deaf

1720 Glendale Milford Road

Cincinnati, Ohio 45215

(513) 771-7600

DESIGN FIRM: The Bradford Lawton Design Group, San Antonio, Texas
ART DIRECTORS/DESIGNERS: Brad Lawton, Jody Laney

Farm to Market

Alan Bland
1133
Austin
Hwy
San
Antonio
Texas
78209
(512)
822-
4450

Farm to Market

Alan Bland
1133
Austin
Hwy
San
Antonio
Texas
78209
(512)
822-
4450

Farm to Market

Alan Bland
1133
Austin
Hwy
San
Antonio
Texas
78209
(512)
822-
4450

Farm to Market

Alan Bland
1133
Austin
Hwy
San
Antonio
Texas
78209
(512)
822-

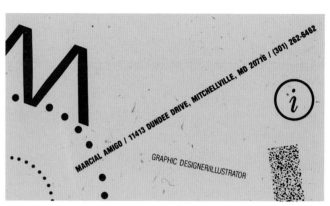

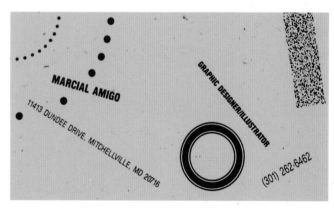

Marcial Amigo

DESIGNER/

ILLUSTRATOR: Marcial

Amigo, Mitchellville,

Maryland

PRINTER: GS Printing

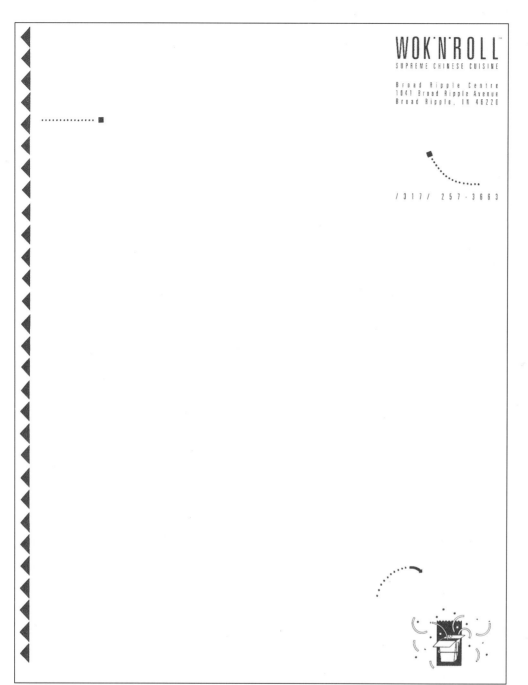

WOK'N'ROLL™
SUPREME CHINESE CUISINE

Broad Ripple Centre
1041 Broad Ripple Avenue
Broad Ripple, IN 46220

/ 3 1 7 /   2 5 7 - 3 6 6 3

WOK'N'ROLL™
SUPREME CHINESE CUISINE

/ 3 1 7 /   2 5 7 - 3 6 6 3

Broad Ripple Centre
1041 Broad Ripple Avenue
Broad Ripple, IN 46220

DESIGN FIRM: Held &

Diedrich Design,

Indianapolis, Indiana

DESIGNER/

ILLUSTRATOR: Tim Gant

Wok 'n' Roll

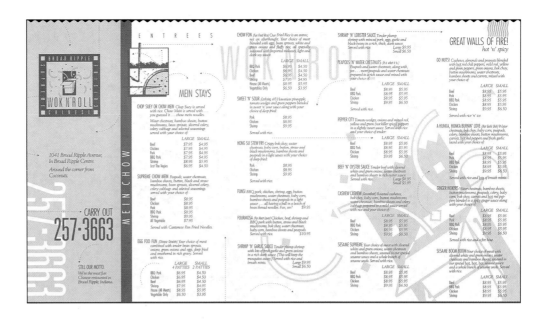

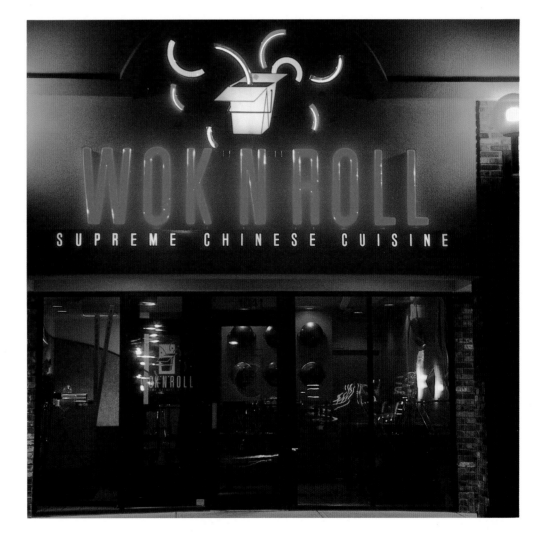

DESIGN FIRM: plus design inc., Boston, Massachusetts
ART DIRECTOR/ DESIGNER: Anita Meyer
ILLUSTRATOR: Nicole Juen

PHILIP'S TOTAL CARE SALON

Vinny Prestipino   34 Charter Street   Hair
                    Boston   Nails
                    Massachusetts 02113 Waxing
                    617-523-8356   Tanning

PHILIP'S TOTAL CARE SALON

Doreen Merola   34 Charter Street   Hair
                 Boston   Nails
                 Massachusetts 02113 Waxing
                 617-523-8356   Tanning

PHILIP'S TOTAL CARE SALON

Phyllis Maderia   34 Charter Street   Hair
                   Boston   Nails
                   Massachusetts 02113 Waxing
                   617-523-8356   Tanning

PHILIP'S TOTAL CARE SALON

Maria Russo   34 Charter Street   Hair
               Boston   Nails
               Massachusetts 02113 Waxing
               617-523-8356   Tanning

Bryan Peterson

207 E. Buffalo, Suite 543
Milwaukee, WI 53202
414-291-0300

DESIGN FIRM: Square Dogs Illustration, Milwaukee, Wisconsin DESIGNERS/ ILLUSTRATORS: Dave Schweitzer, Bryan Peterson, Peter Wells

Square Dogs Illustration

Bryan Peterson

207 E. Buffalo, Suite 543
Milwaukee, WI 53202
414-291-0300
FAX: 414-272-6996

Dave Schweitzer

207 E. Buffalo, Suite 543
Milwaukee, WI 53202
414-272-5666
FAX: 414-272-6996

Peter Wells

207 E. Buffalo, Suite 543
Milwaukee, WI 53202
414-272-5525
FAX: 414-272-6996

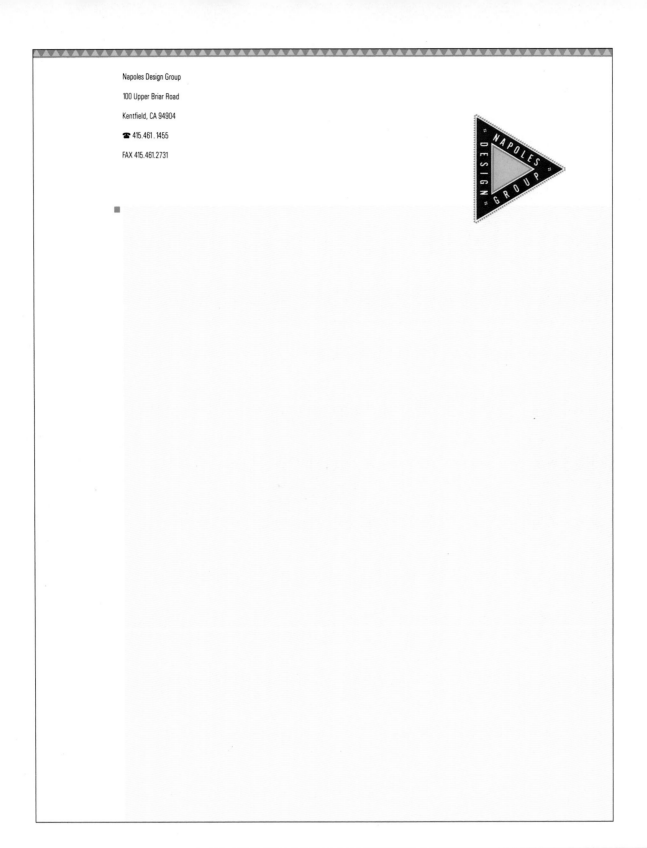

Napoles Design Group

100 Upper Briar Road

Kentfield, CA 94904

☎ 415.461.1455

FAX 415.461.2731

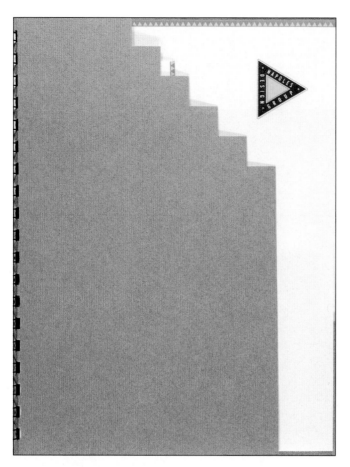

Veronica Napoles

Principal

Napoles Design Group

100 Upper Briar Road

Kentfield, CA 94904

☎ 415.461.1455

FAX 415.461.2731

DESIGN FIRM: Napoles

Design Group, Kentfield,

California

ART DIRECTOR:

Veronica Napoles

DESIGNERS: Veronica

Napoles, Karyn Kraft

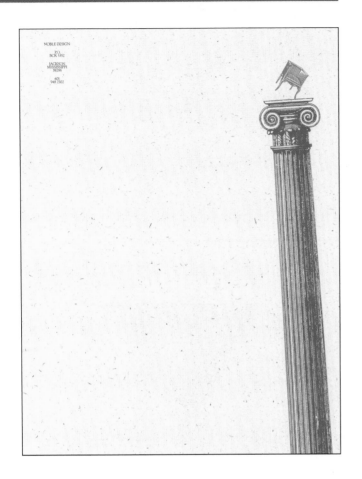

DESIGN FIRM: Larry

Smith & Associates,

Decatur, Georgia

DESIGNER: Robin

Wineman

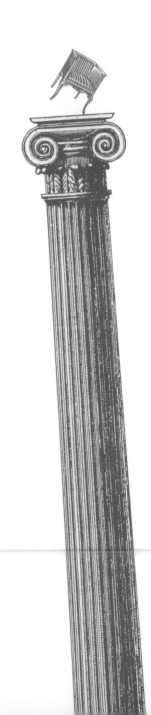

Proyecto de Poder
Trabajador Agrícola
Farmworker Power Project
120 S. Elizabeth
Pueblo, Colorado 81004
P.O. Box 2760
Denver, Colorado 80201

Proyecto de Poder Trabajador Agrícola
Farmworker Power Project
120 S. Elizabeth   Pueblo, Colorado 81004
P.O. Box 2760   Denver, Colorado 80201

Proyecto de Poder Trabajador Agrícola   Farmworker Power Project
120 S. Elizabeth   Pueblo, Colorado 81004   P.O. Box 2760   Denver, Colorado 80201

Farmworker Power Project

DESIGN FIRM: Davis

Design, Denver, Colorado

DESIGNER: Monique

Davis

ILLUSTRATOR: Tony

Ortega

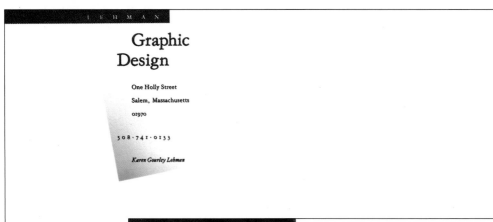

DESIGN FIRM: Lehman Graphic Design, Salem, Massachusetts
DESIGNER: Karen Gourley Lehman
PRINTER: Espo Litho, Inc.

LEHMAN

Graphic
Design

One Holly Street
Salem, Massachusetts
01970

508·741·0133

Karen Gourley Lehman

LEHMAN

Graphic
Design

One Holly Street
Salem, Massachusetts
01970

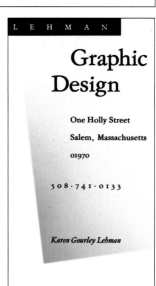

LEHMAN

Graphic
Design

One Holly Street
Salem, Massachusetts
01970

508·741·0133

Karen Gourley Lehman

Carlos Alejandro
Photography
8 East 37th St.
Wilmington, DE
19802 · 2321
302 · 762 · 8220

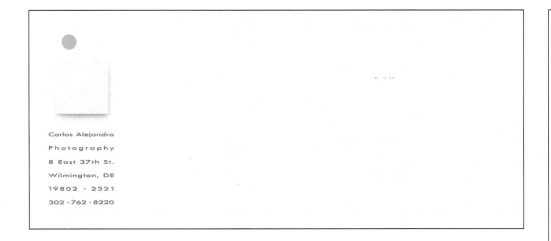

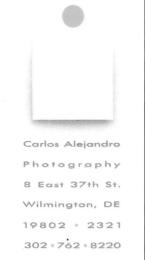

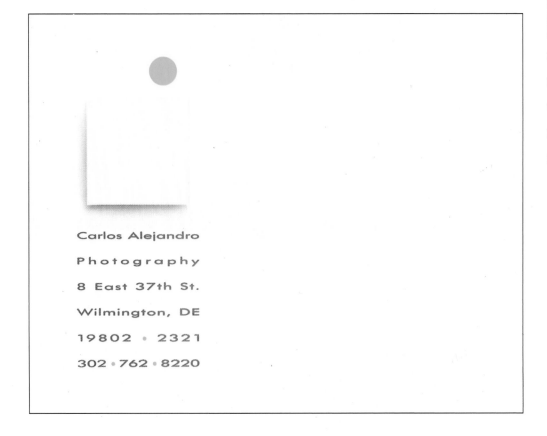

DESIGNER: Ingrid

Hansen-Lynch,

Wilmington, Delaware

ILLUSTRATOR: John

Francis

Kevin Akers

DESIGNER/

ILLUSTRATOR: Kevin

Akers, San Francisco,

California

Patricia McClear

DESIGN FIRM: McClear

Studios, Colchester,

Connecticut

ART DIRECTOR/

DESIGNER: Patricia

McClear

DESIGN FIRM: Art

Lofgreen Design,

Phoenix, Arizona

DESIGNER: Art Lofgreen

G.M. Boshara, Inc. (Interior Design)

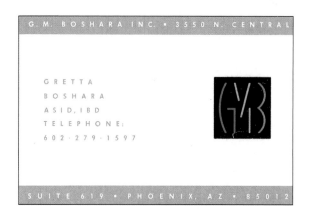

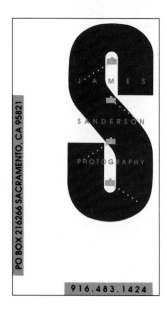

PO BOX 216266 SACRAMENTO, CA 95821

916.483.1424

POST OFFICE BOX 216266 SACRAMENTO, CALIFORNIA 95821

916.483.1424

DESIGN FIRM: Wiley

Design, Sacramento,

California

ART DIRECTOR: Jean

Wiley

DESIGNER: Elizabeth

Ingebretsen

James Sanderson (Photographer)

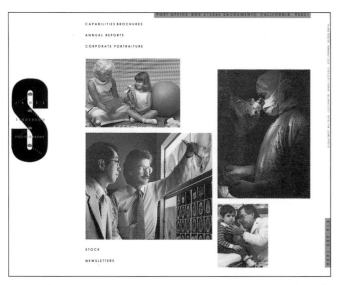

Charles Greacen
Illustration & Graphics

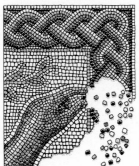

1808 Richardson Place
Tampa, Florida 33606
(813) 251-1944

Charles Greacen
Illustration & Graphics

1808 Richardson Place
Tampa, Florida 33606
(813) 251-1944

Charles Greacen
Illustration & Graphics

1808 Richardson Place
Tampa, Florida 33606
(813) 251-1944

DESIGN FIRM: Charles Greacen Illustration & Graphics, Tampa, Florida
ILLUSTRATOR: Charles Greacen

DESIGN FIRM: Nautilus

Design, Inc., Wolfeboro,

New Hampshire

ART DIRECTOR/

DESIGNER: Bill Wilkens

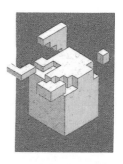

Marcy L. Weeks (Trade Show/Event Management)

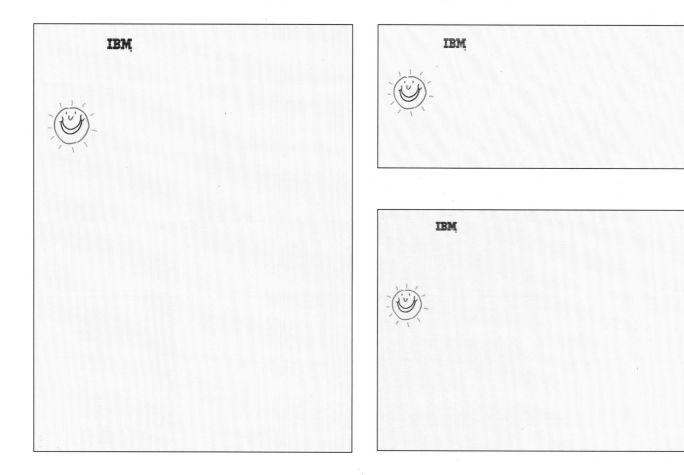

Ser El Mejor / Ser O Melhor

IBM.
Convención Latinoamericana
Convenção Latinoamericana

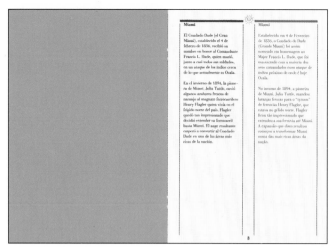

DESIGN FIRM: Lopez
Salpeter & Associates,
New York, New York
ART DIRECTOR: Bob
Salpeter
ILLUSTRATOR: Alex
Tiani

D A V I D É ♦ F U R

330 SEVENTH AVENUE
CORNER OF 29TH STREET
NEW YORK CITY 10001
212 ♦ 268 ♦ 0050

D A V I D É ♦ F U R

330 SEVENTH AVENUE / CORNER OF 29TH STREET ♦

NEW YORK CITY ♦ 10001 ♦ 212-268-0050

Davidé Fur

DESIGN FIRM: Louey/

Rubino Design Group,

Santa Monica, California

ART DIRECTOR: Regina

Rubino

DESIGNER/

ILLUSTRATOR: Robert

Louey

Johnson

Productions

8035

Broadway

San Antonio

Texas

78209

512   829   4200
San Antonio

214   869   4414
Dallas

512   829   4266
Fax

J O H N S O N

DESIGN FIRM: Taylor/

Christian Advertising,

Inc., San Antonio, Texas

DESIGNER/

ILLUSTRATOR: Mark

Wilson

Johnson Productions (Film)

Neverne K. Covington (Artist)

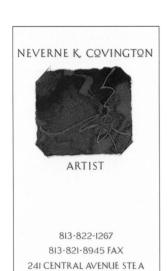

ART DIRECTOR: Lisa Hill,
St. Petersburg, Florida
DESIGNERS: Lisa Hill,
Neverne Covington
ILLUSTRATOR: Neverne
Covington

100

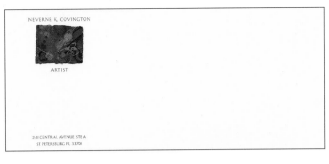

NEVERNE K. COVINGTON

ARTIST

813-822-1267
813-821-8945 FAX
241 CENTRAL AVENUE STE A
ST. PETERSBURG FL 33701

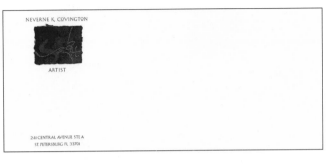

2-41 CENTRAL AVENUE STE A
ST. PETERSBURG FL 33701

NEVERNE K. COVINGTON

ARTIST

2-41 CENTRAL AVENUE STE A
ST. PETERSBURG FL 33701

NEVERNE K. COVINGTON

ARTIST

2-41 CENTRAL AVENUE STE A
ST. PETERSBURG FL 33701

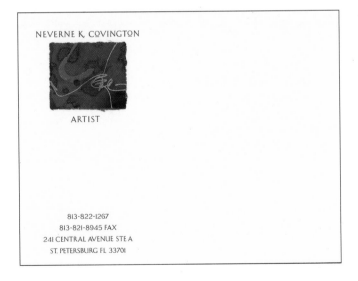

NEVERNE K. COVINGTON

ARTIST

813-822-1267
813-821-8945 FAX
241 CENTRAL AVENUE STE A
ST. PETERSBURG FL 33701

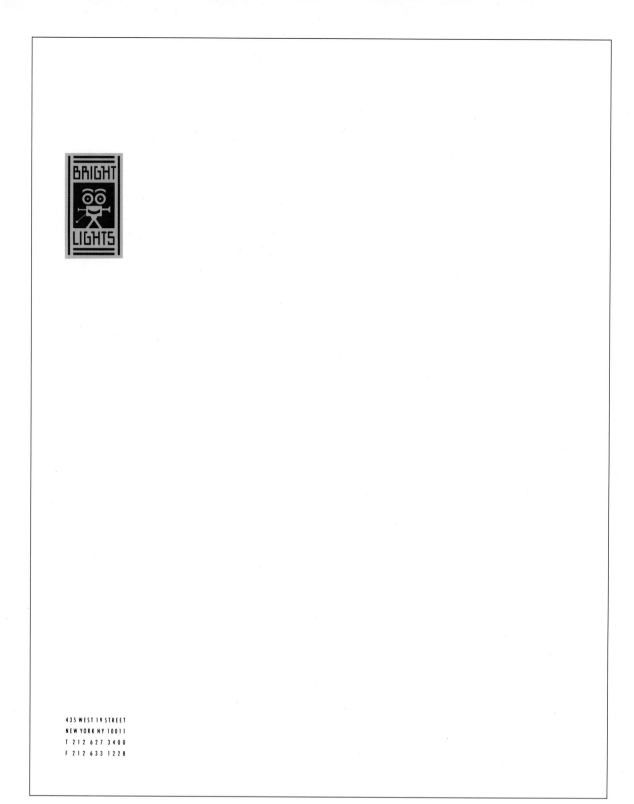

435 WEST 19 STREET
NEW YORK NY 10011
T 212 627 3400
F 212 633 1228

VICTOR GOSS

DIRECTOR

CINEMATOGRAPHER

DESIGN FIRM:

Pentagram Design,

New York, New York

DESIGNER: Woody Pirtle

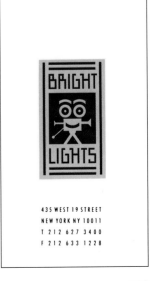

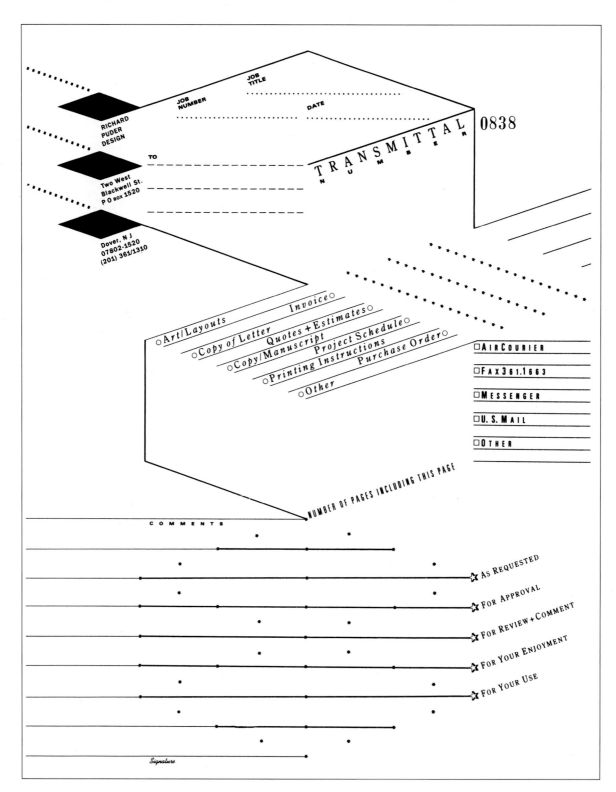

JOB TITLE

JOB NUMBER

DATE

RICHARD
PUDER
DESIGN

TO

Two West
Blackwell St.
P O box 1520

Dover, NJ
07802-1520
(201) 361/1310

TRANSMITTAL NUMBER 0838

○Art/Layouts   Invoice○
  ○Copy of Letter   Quotes+Estimates○
    ○Copy/Manuscript   Project Schedule○
      ○Printing Instructions   Purchase Order○
        ○Other

☐ AIR COURIER

☐ FAX 361.1663

☐ MESSENGER

☐ U. S. MAIL

☐ OTHER

NUMBER OF PAGES INCLUDING THIS PAGE

COMMENTS

☆ AS REQUESTED

☆ FOR APPROVAL

☆ FOR REVIEW + COMMENT

☆ FOR YOUR ENJOYMENT

☆ FOR YOUR USE

Signature

DESIGN FIRM: Richard   **DESIGNERS: Richard**

Puder Design, Dover,   **Puder, Lee Grabarczyk**

New Jersey

Richard Puder Design

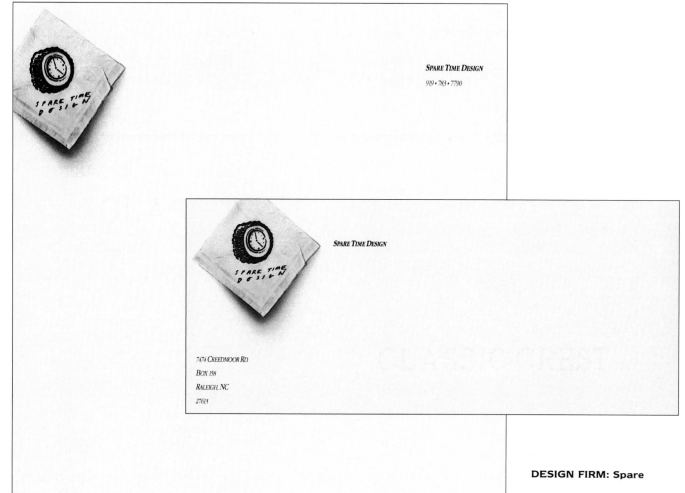

DESIGN FIRM: Spare Time Design, Raleigh, North Carolina
ART DIRECTORS/ DESIGNERS: Patrick Short, Todd Coats
ILLUSTRATOR: Todd Coats

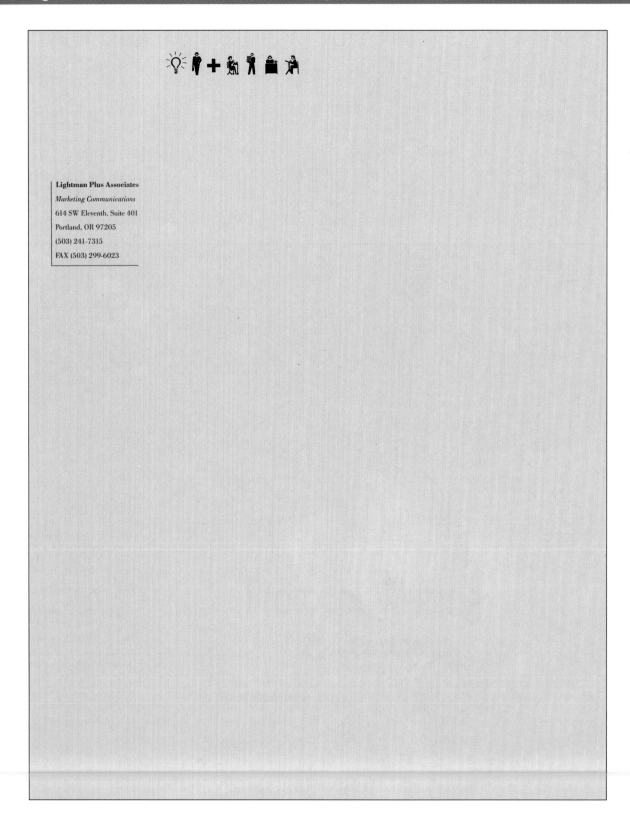

Lightman Plus Associates

Marketing Communications

614 SW Eleventh, Suite 401

Portland, OR 97205

(503) 241-7315

FAX (503) 299-6023

Lightman Plus Associates

Marketing Communications

614 SW Eleventh, Suite 401

Portland, OR 97205

(503) 241-7315

FAX (503) 299-6023

Robert Lightman

Lightman Plus Associates

Marketing Communications

614 SW Eleventh, Suite 401

Portland, OR 97205

DESIGN FIRM:

Smithgroup, Inc.,

Portland, Oregon

ART DIRECTOR: Thom

Smith

DESIGNERS: Thom

Smith, Gregg

Frederickson

Lightman Plus Associates

Marketing Communications

614 SW Eleventh, Suite 401

Portland, OR 97205

g.russ
IMAGES

906 East 5th St.
Austin TX 78702
(512) 478-4478

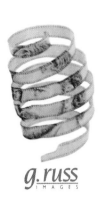

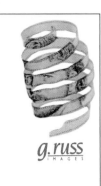

g.russ
I M A G E S

gary russ
photographer

906 East 5th St.
Austin TX 78702
(512) 478-4478

g.russ
I M A G E S

906 East 5th St.
Austin TX 78702
(512) 478-4478

DESIGN FIRM: RCR & Co.,

Austin, Texas

DESIGNER: Curtis Riker

ILLUSTRATOR: Gary

McElhaney

D.C.

DEAN CHANCE CREATIVE

COPYWRITING,
PRODUCTION SERVICES
AND INTERESTING IDEAS
FOR STUFF.

D.C.

D.C.

3576 MCKINLEY BLVD.
SUITE 100
SACRAMENTO, CA 95816
(916) 457-3522

DESIGN FIRM: Elizabeth Mekjavich Graphic Design, Sacramento, California

ART DIRECTOR/ COPYWRITER: Dean Chance

DESIGNER: Elizabeth Mekjavich

ILLUSTRATOR: Brian Walima

Dean Chance Creative (Copywriter)

A store providing
wedding consulting,
party rentals, and
supplies.

DESIGN FIRM:

Armstrong Image Group,

Santa Rosa, California

ART DIRECTORS: Tom

Armstrong, Deborah

Cunninghame-Blank

DESIGNER/

ILLUSTRATOR: Deborah

Cunninghame-Blank

TERRY E. McLEAN, M.D.
DIRECTOR

PETER C. BOYLAN, M.D.

DAVID A. TILLEMA, M.D.

ROBERT J. TAKACS, M.D.

DESIGN FIRM: Kuhn & Wittenborn, Kansas City, Missouri
DESIGNER: Randy Robinson

ROCKHILL MEDICAL PLAZA NORTH

6650 TROOST, SUITE 103

KANSAS CITY, MISSOURI 64131

PHONE: (816) 926-BACK

(800) 798-2235

ROCKHILL MEDICAL PLAZA NORTH

6650 TROOST, SUITE 103

KANSAS CITY, MISSOURI 64131

DEBORAH H. KIMBALL, Ph.D.
ADMINISTRATIVE DIRECTOR

(816) 926-BACK
(800) 798-2235

ROCKHILL MEDICAL PLAZA NORTH
6650 TROOST, SUITE 103
KANSAS CITY, MISSOURI 64131

Kansas City Spine Center

STEPHEN KOWALSKI DESIGNWORKS

2550 Ninth Street
Suite 208A
Berkeley, California 94710
Telephone: 415·548·2185
Fax: 415·548·2187

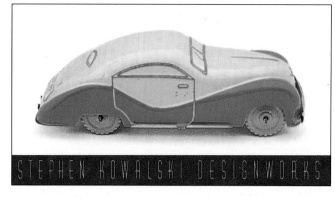

STEPHEN KOWALSKI DESIGNWORKS

2550 Ninth Street · Suite 208A

Berkeley, California 94710

Telephone: 415·548·2185

Fax: 415·548·2187

Classic Graphic Design

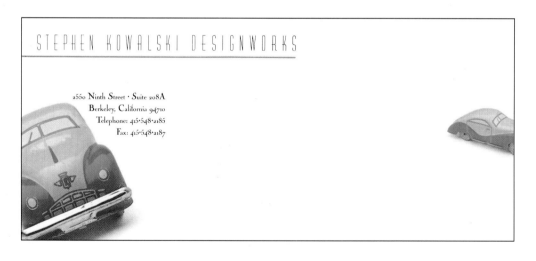

STEPHEN KOWALSKI DESIGNWORKS

2550 Ninth Street · Suite 208A
Berkeley, California 94710
Telephone: 415·548·2185
Fax: 415·548·2187

DESIGN FIRM: Stephen

Kowalski Designworks,

Berkeley, California

DESIGNER: Stephen

Kowalski

PHOTOGRAPHER:

George Post

JULIA TALCOTT
617-232-7306

38 Linden Street
Brookline, MA 02146

DESIGNER/

ILLUSTRATOR: Julia

Talcott, Brookline,

Massachusetts

JULIA TALCOTT
617-232-7306

38 Linden Street
Brookline, MA
02146

Julia Talcott Illustration

Burton Morris is an
illustrator and Denise
Hixenbaugh is an artists
representative.
DESIGNER/
ILLUSTRATOR: Burton
Morris, Pittsburgh,
Pennsylvania

Burton Morris/Denise Hixenbaugh

John Kneapler Design

I'm John Kneapler, the one on the left.
Graphic/Corporate Design. 48 West 21st 12th Fl.
New York, New York 10010 (212) 463-9774

DESIGN FIRM: John Kneapler Design, New York, New York

DESIGNER: John Kneapler

PHOTOGRAPHER: Charles Kneapler

House of Games

HOUSE
of
GAMES

South Street Seaport
11 Fulton Street
New York, NY 10038
212-571-3135

DESIGN FIRM: Tippit Woolworth Design, New York, New York

DESIGNER: Carol Tippit Woolworth

Earthly Pleasures

DESIGN FIRM: Kiku Obata & Company, St. Louis, Missouri

ART DIRECTORS: Kiku Obata, Teresa Bollwerk

DESIGNER: Teresa Bollwerk

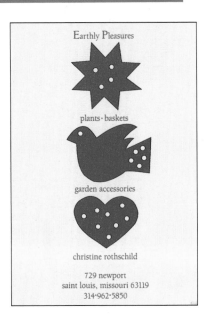

Earthly Pleasures

plants · baskets

garden accessories

christine rothschild

729 newport
saint louis, missouri 63119
314·962·5850

117

THE DANDY CANDY MAN

Purveyor of Condommints

•

POST OFFICE BOX 2151
LOS GATOS, CA 95031
PHONE · 408.378.5600
TELEFAX · 408.354.1450

RICK THARP
HEAD DANDY MAN

THE DANDY CANDY MAN

Purveyor of Condommints

•

POST OFFICE BOX 2151
LOS GATOS, CA 95031
PHONE · 408.378.5600
TELEFAX · 408.354.1450

DESIGN FIRM: Tharp Did It, Los Gatos, California
DESIGNER: Rick Tharp
ILLUSTRATOR: Kim Tomlinson

The Dandy Candy Man

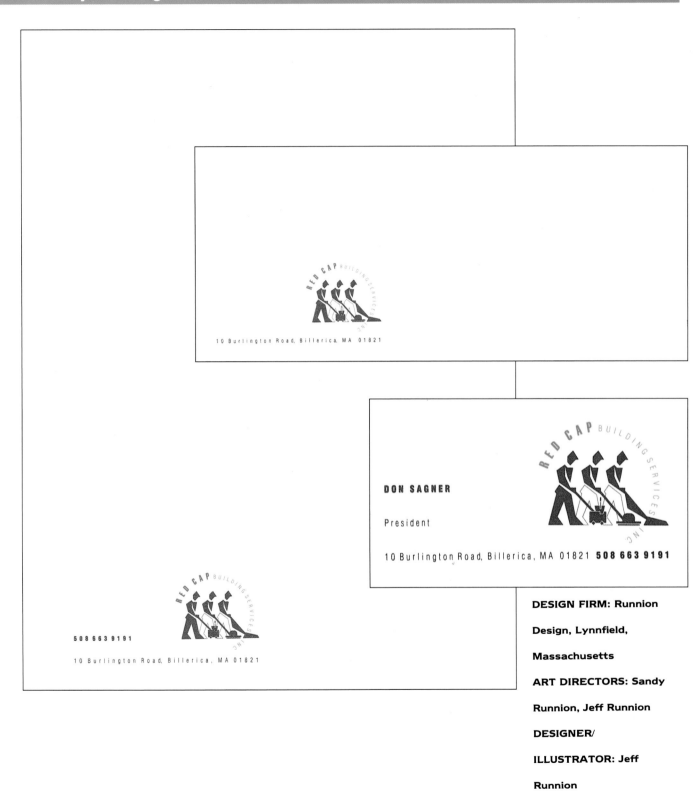

10 Burlington Road, Billerica, MA 01821

DON SAGNER

President

10 Burlington Road, Billerica, MA 01821 **508 663 9191**

508 663 9191

10 Burlington Road, Billerica, MA 01821

**DESIGN FIRM: Runnion
Design, Lynnfield,
Massachusetts
ART DIRECTORS: Sandy
Runnion, Jeff Runnion
DESIGNER/
ILLUSTRATOR: Jeff
Runnion**

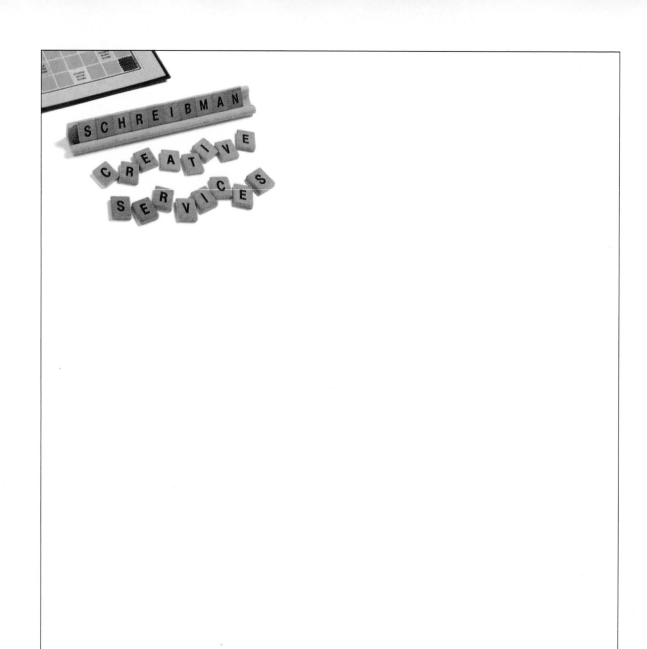

1102 17th Avenue S. • Suite 200 • Nashville, TN 37212 • (615) 321-3512

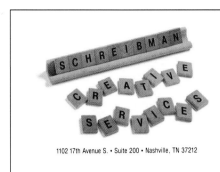

1102 17th Avenue S. • Suite 200 • Nashville, TN 37212

JANET SCHREIBMAN

1102 17th Avenue S. • Suite 200 • Nashville, TN 37212 • (615) 321-3512

DESIGN FIRM: Katherine

DeVault Design,

Nashville, Tennessee

ART DIRECTOR/

DESIGNER: Katherine

DeVault

PHOTOGRAPHER: Jim

DeVault

CREATIVE THAT WORKS ACROSS THE BOARD

ART DIRECTOR/

DESIGNER: Penny

Redfern, Pasadena,

California

PHOTOGRAPHER:

Michael Fineman

Penny Redfern

244 East Lake Dr., Atlanta, Georgia 30317, (404) 377-8490

Penny Redfern

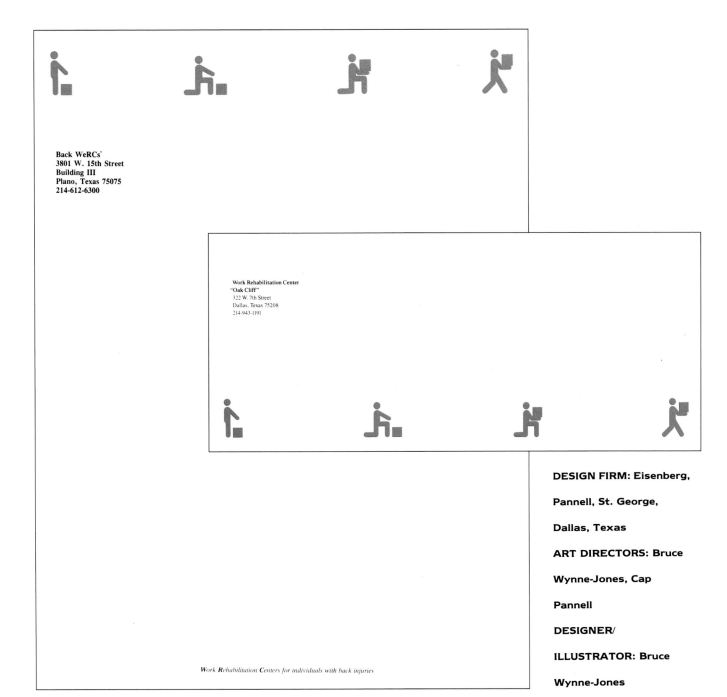

Back WeRCs®
3801 W. 15th Street
Building III
Plano, Texas 75075
214-612-6300

Work Rehabilitation Center
"Oak Cliff"
322 W. 7th Street
Dallas, Texas 75208
214-943-1191

Work Rehabilitation Centers for individuals with back injuries

DESIGN FIRM: Eisenberg, Pannell, St. George, Dallas, Texas

ART DIRECTORS: Bruce Wynne-Jones, Cap Pannell

DESIGNER/ ILLUSTRATOR: Bruce Wynne-Jones

A L A M O • H E I G H T S • P E T • C L I N I C
0 9 • K 9 • F E L I N E

A L A M O • H E I G H T S • P E T • C L I N I C
0 9 • K 9 • F E L I N E

6488 N. New Braunfels • San Antonio, Texas 78209

6488 N. New Braunfels • San Antonio, Texas 78209 • (512) 821-5544

DESIGN FIRM: Taylor/

Christian Advertising,

San Antonio, Texas

ART DIRECTOR: Roger

Christian

ILLUSTRATOR: Karen

Hudson

DESIGN FIRM: Lipetz

Design, Seattle,

Washington

DESIGNER: Jan Lipetz

ILLUSTRATOR: Jud

Guitteau

2867 S.W. MONTGOMERY DR • PORTLAND OR 97201 • (503) 226-3611

2867 S.W. MONTGOMERY DR. • PORTLAND, OR 97201 • (503) 226-3611

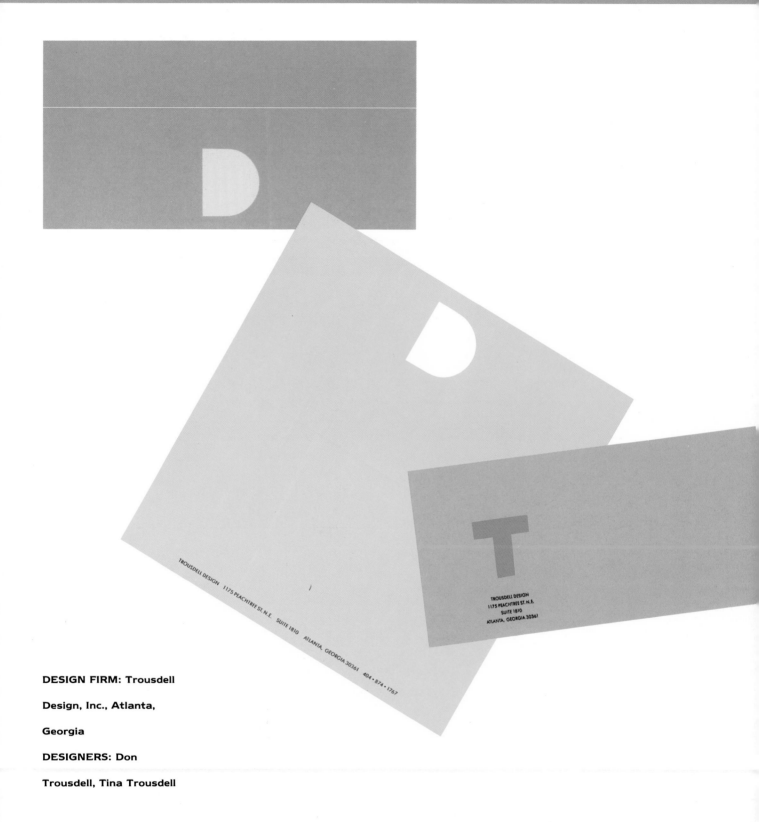

DESIGN FIRM: Trousdell

Design, Inc., Atlanta,

Georgia

DESIGNERS: Don

Trousdell, Tina Trousdell

126

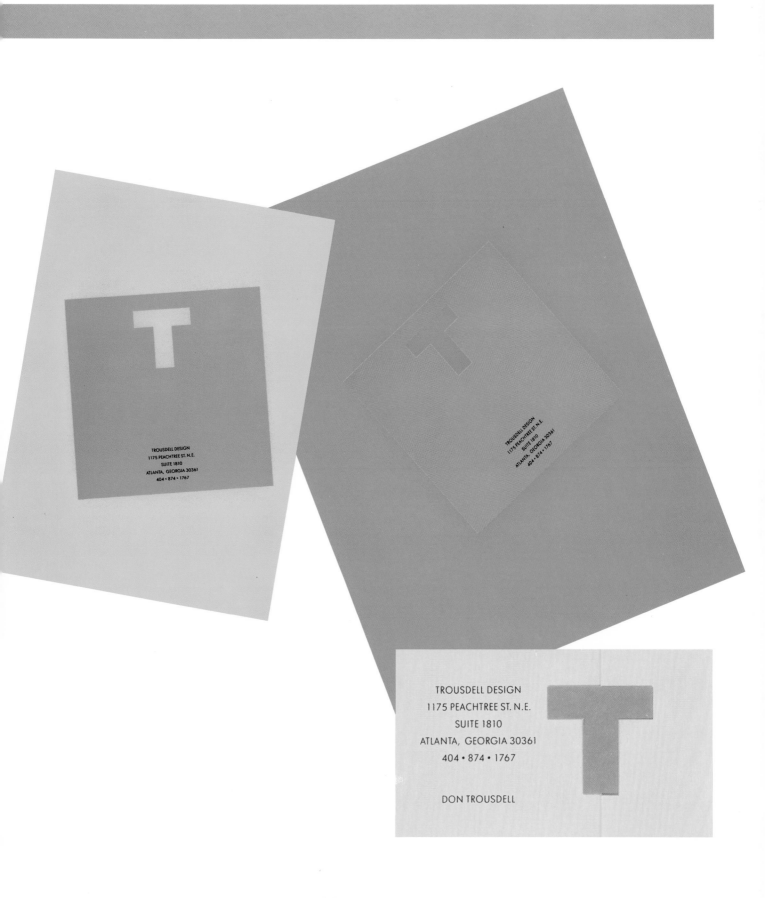

TROUSDELL DESIGN
1175 PEACHTREE ST. N.E.
SUITE 1810
ATLANTA, GEORGIA 30361
404 • 874 • 1767

TROUSDELL DESIGN
1175 PEACHTREE ST. N.E.
SUITE 1810
ATLANTA, GEORGIA 30361
404 • 874 • 1767

DON TROUSDELL

3846 Dight Avenue South, Minneapolis, Minnesota 55406. Phone (612) 721-2408, Fax (612) 721-2329, Toll Free 1-800-237-5520.

Lake Street Shirts

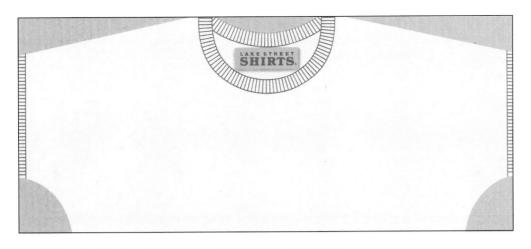

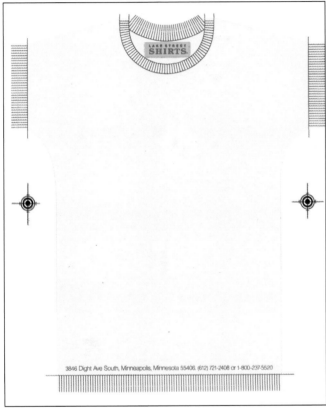

DESIGN FIRM: Sue
Crolick Advertising &
Design, Minneapolis,
Minnesota
DESIGNERS: Sue Crolick,
Patt Sizer
COPYWRITER: Nancy
Johnson

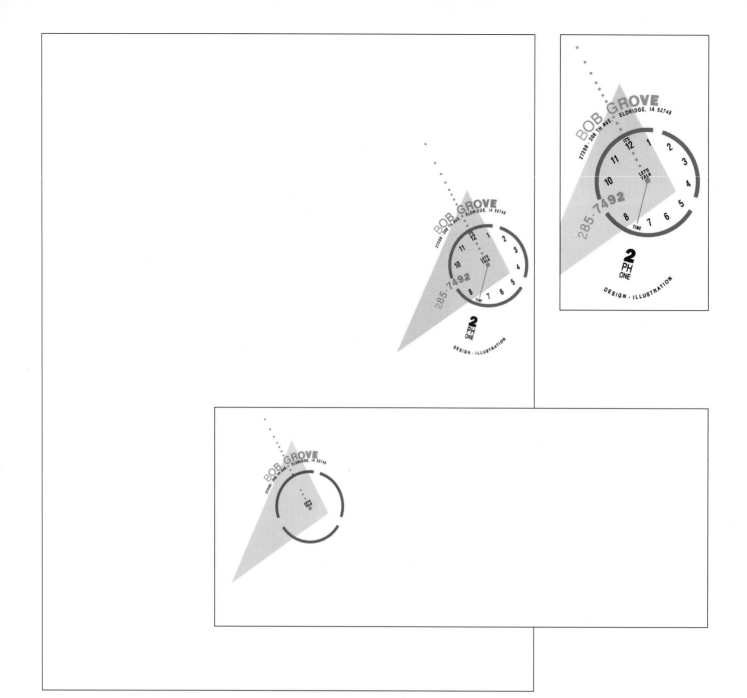

Bob Grove Design & Illustration

DESIGNER/

ILLUSTRATOR: Bob

Grove, Davenport, Iowa

DESIGN FIRM: Tracy

Sabin Illustration &

Design, San Diego,

California

DESIGNER/

ILLUSTRATOR: Tracy

Sabin

My friend Marie said,
"Little Designs!
What kind of name
is that?
Ya gotta think big.
You're a graphic
designer working on all
sorts of projects –
logos, brochures, posters,
annual reports.
If you think big,
you'll get the big
assignments.
Like revamping the
Victoria's Secret catalog.
Or clean-up
an ad campaign
for Exxon.
Then there is
dictating the ongoing
Trump signage
projects.
Or how about
designing the packaging
for cold fusion
generators..."

Sorry Marie.

Little Designs
129 Butler Avenue
Providence
Rhode Island 02903
401-861-5559

Date

Little Designs

Little Designs
129 Butler Avenue
Providence
Rhode Island 02903
401-861-5559

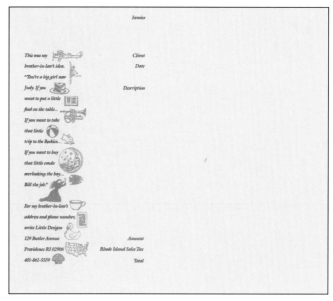

Invoice

*This was my
brother-in-law's idea.
"You're a big girl now
Judy. If you
want to put a little
food on the table…
If you want to take
that little
trip to the Rockies…
If you want to buy
that little condo
overlooking the bay…
Bill the job."*

*For my brother-in-law's
address and phone number,
write Little Designs
129 Butler Avenue
Providence RI 02906
401-861-5559*

Client

Date

Description

Amount

Rhode Island Sales Tax

Total

**DESIGN FIRM: Little
Designs, Providence,
Rhode Island
DESIGNER: Judy Little**

Little Designs
Yes, I do projects
of all shapes and
sizes.
My name is
Judy Little.
I'm a graphic
designer.
Hence the name…

Little Designs
129 Butler Ave
Providence Rhode Island 02906
401-861-5559

Little Designs
129 Butler Avenue
Providence RI 02906

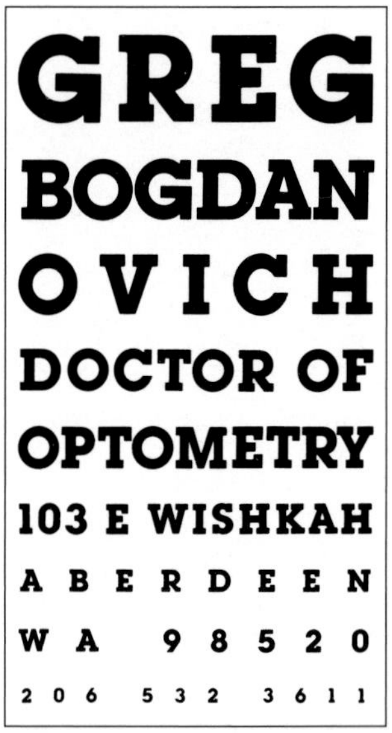

GREG
BOGDAN
OVICH
DOCTOR OF
OPTOMETRY
103 E WISHKAH
ABERDEEN
WA 98520
206 532 3611

GREG
BOGDAN
OVICH
DOCTOR OF
OPTOMETRY
103 E WISHKAH
ABERDEEN
WA 98520
206 532 3611

Greg Bogdanovich (Optometrist)

DESIGN FIRM: Angela

Turk Art & Copy,

Mountlake Terrace,

Washington

ART DIRECTOR/

DESIGNER: Angela Turk

Helen Greening & Associates, Inc.
Specializing In Personnel Growth
For Bakeries
3703 Douglas Drive
Minneapolis, MN 55422
(612) 537-9321

Helen Greening

DESIGN FIRM: Behr-Lemons, Minneapolis, Minnesota

DESIGNER: Brenda Behr

PHOTOGRAPHER: Bill Gale

6114 WINDSOR MILL ROAD   SUITE 200   BALTIMORE, MARYLAND 21207

Graphic Gofers (Messenger Service)

6314 WINDSOR MILL ROAD   SUITE 200   BALTIMORE, MARYLAND 21207

DESIGN FIRM: Cooper

Wingard Design,

Baltimore, Maryland

DESIGNER/

ILLUSTRATOR: JoAnne

Cooper Wingard

PRINTER: Agnihotra

Press, Inc.

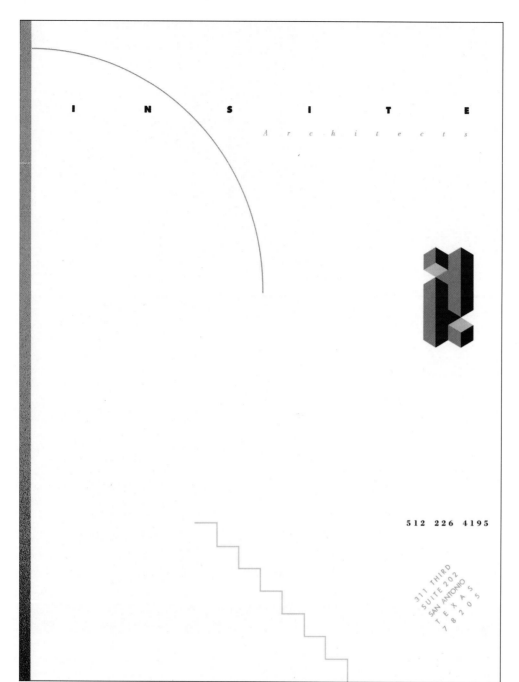

DESIGN FIRM: Taylor/
Christian Advertising,
Inc., San Antonio, Texas
**DESIGNER/
ILLUSTRATOR:** Mark
Wilcox

Insite Architects

DESIGN FIRM: NAG

Design, Houston, Texas

DESIGNER: Neva Alford

ILLUSTRATOR: Bill

Nelson

SUSAN GRILL JOSS
GRAPHIC DESIGN
ILLUSTRATION

404 • 872 • 9619

1740 N. PELHAM ROAD, NE
ATLANTA, GEORGIA 30324

Susan Grill Joss Graphic Design/Illustration

SUSAN GRILL JOSS
GRAPHIC DESIGN
ILLUSTRATION

404 • 872 • 9619

1740 N. PELHAM ROAD, NE
ATLANTA, GEORGIA 30324

SUSAN GRILL JOSS
GRAPHIC DESIGN
ILLUSTRATION

404 • 872 • 9619

1740 N. PELHAM ROAD, NE
ATLANTA, GEORGIA 30324

SUSAN GRILL JOSS
GRAPHIC DESIGN
ILLUSTRATION

404 • 872 • 9619

1740 N. PELHAM ROAD, NE
ATLANTA, GEORGIA 30324

DESIGN FIRM: Susan
Grill Joss Graphic Design/
Illustration, Atlanta,
Georgia
DESIGNER: Susan Grill
Joss

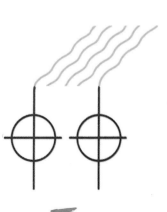

Corporate Communications

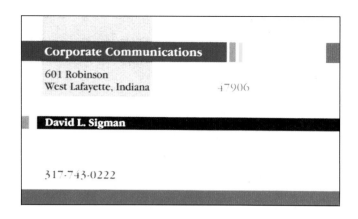

Corporate Communications

601 Robinson
West Lafayette, Indiana   47906

David L. Sigman

317-743-0222

DESIGN FIRM: Corporate

Communications, West

Lafayette, Indiana

ART DIRECTOR: David L.

Sigman

Robin's Cookie Works

DESIGN FIRM: Dix &

Eaton, Erie, Pennsylvania

DESIGNER: Chuck

Benson

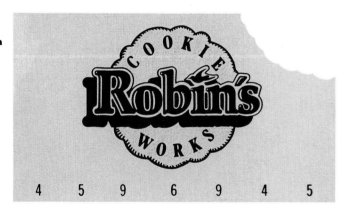

4   5   9   6   9   4   5

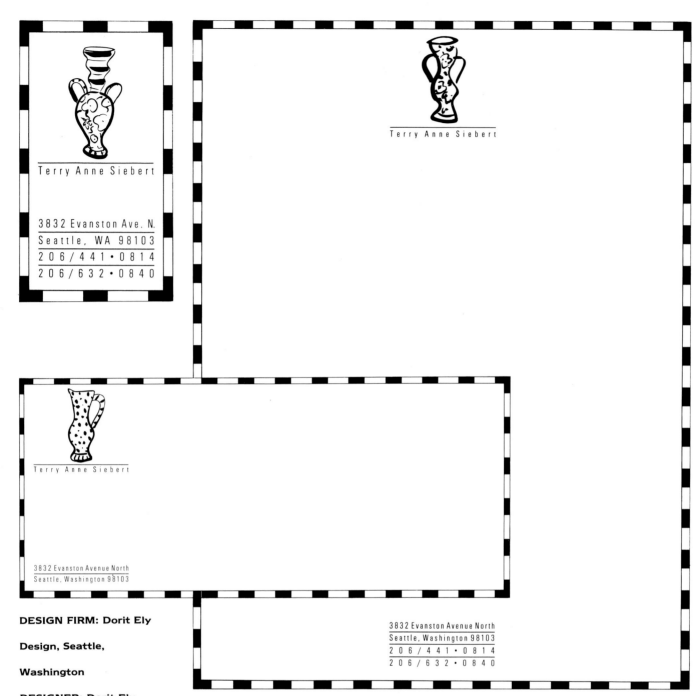

Terry Anne Siebert

3832 Evanston Ave. N.
Seattle, WA 98103
206/441•0814
206/632•0840

Terry Anne Siebert

3832 Evanston Avenue North
Seattle, Washington 98103

3832 Evanston Avenue North
Seattle, Washington 98103
206/441•0814
206/632•0840

DESIGN FIRM: Dorit Ely

Design, Seattle,

Washington

DESIGNER: Dorit Ely

ILLUSTRATOR: Terry

Anne Siebert

Terry Anne Siebert (Ceramic Artist)

2345-A HARPER STREET · JACKSONVILLE, FLORIDA 32204

DESIGN FIRM: Robin Shepherd Studios, Jacksonville, Florida

ART DIRECTORS: Robin Shepherd, Tom Schifanella

ILLUSTRATORS: Mike Barnhart, Bob Cooper

**DESIGN FIRM: Arts &
Letters Ltd., Falls Church,
Virginia**
**ART DIRECTOR: Susan
Eder**
**DESIGNER/
ILLUSTRATOR: Craig
Dennis**

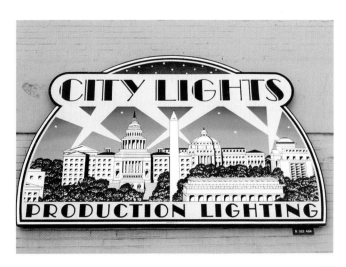

Elaine M. Brill
President

242 N. Remington Road
Bexley, Ohio 43209

242 N. Remington Road
Bexley, Ohio 43209
614/236-1740

Scripts & Concepts, Inc.

Elaine M. Brill
President

242 N. Remington Road
Bexley, Ohio 43209
614/236-1740

DESIGN FIRM:

Rickabaugh Graphics,

Columbus, Ohio

ART DIRECTORS: Eric

Rickabaugh, Mark

Krumel

DESIGNER/

ILLUSTRATOR: Mark

Krumel

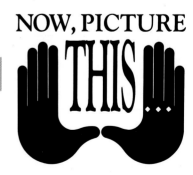

DEPARTURE FILMS, INC.
2309 WYCLIFF STREET
SUITE SEVEN
SAINT PAUL
MINNESOTA
5   5   1   4
612 - 646 - 3622
FAX 612-646-3577

DEPARTURE FILMS, INC.
2309 WYCLIFF STREET
SUITE SEVEN
SAINT PAUL
MINNESOTA
5   5   1   4

DEPARTURE FILMS, INC.
2309 WYCLIFF STREET
SUITE SEVEN
SAINT PAUL
MINNESOTA
5   5   1   4
612 - 646 - 3622
FAX 612-646-3577

DESIGN FIRM: Designed Marketing, Minneapolis, Minnesota
DESIGNER/ ILLUSTRATOR: Tim Moran

DINOSAURS ALIVE!
at the Austin Nature Center

301 Nature Center Drive · Austin, Texas 78746 · (512) 327-8180

DESIGN FIRM: Klassen Graphic Designs, Austin, Texas

ART DIRECTOR: Alison Klassen

DESIGNER/ILLUSTRATOR: Claire English

Austin Nature Center

TEAM DESIGN

DIANN BISSELL
JANET BRUSCATO
BOB GRINDELAND

Tower Building
7th and Olive
Suite 500
Seattle
Washington
98101
206-623-1044
FAX Number:
206-625-0154

TEAM DESIGN

Tower Building
7th and Olive
Suite 500
Seattle
Washington
98101

BOB GRINDELAND
Principal

TEAM DESIGN

Tower Building

7th and Olive

Suite 500

Seattle

Washington

98101

206-623-1044

FAX Number:

206-625-0154

Team Design

TRUSTWORTHY. LOYAL. HELPFUL. FRIENDLY. COURTEOUS. CHEERFUL. THRIFTY. BRAVE. CLEAN. REVERENT. TOTALLY COOL...AND ALL MOVED IN.

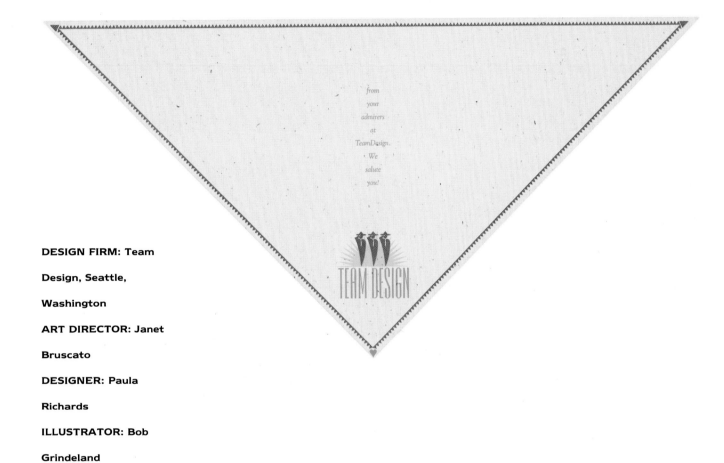

from your admirers at TeamDesign. We salute you!

DESIGN FIRM: Team Design, Seattle, Washington

ART DIRECTOR: Janet Bruscato

DESIGNER: Paula Richards

ILLUSTRATOR: Bob Grindeland

T   E   A   M   —   D   E   S   I   G   N

DESIGN FIRM: Richard
Harrington Illustration,
Rochester, New York
ART DIRECTOR/
ILLUSTRATOR: Richard
Harrington

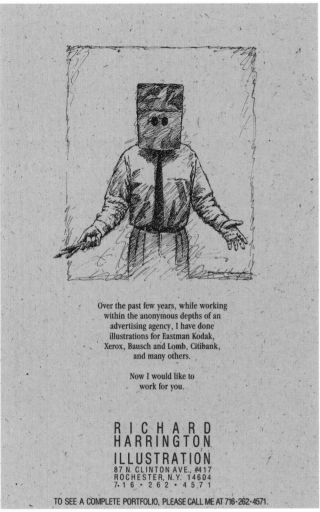

Over the past few years, while working
within the anonymous depths of an
advertising agency, I have done
illustrations for Eastman Kodak,
Xerox, Bausch and Lomb, Citibank,
and many others.

Now I would like to
work for you.

RICHARD
HARRINGTON
ILLUSTRATION
87 N. CLINTON AVE., #417
ROCHESTER, N.Y. 14604
7.1 6 · 2 6 2 · 4 5,7 1

TO SEE A COMPLETE PORTFOLIO, PLEASE CALL ME AT 716·262·4571.

DESIGN FIRM: No Dogs

Design, Boston,

Massachusetts

DESIGNER: Robin

Jareaux

6 1 7 • 5 2 4 • 3 0 9 9
2 8 E L I O T S T R E E T
J A M A I C A P L A I N , M A
0 2 1 3 0 • 2 7 5 7

No Dogs Design

Angela Prather

Tom Hair Marketing Design
····················
2700 Fairmount, Suite 500
Dallas, Texas 75201
····················
214 871 2105

Tom Hair Marketing Design
····················
2700 Fairmount, Suite 500
Dallas, Texas 75201
····················
214 871 2105

DESIGN FIRM: Tom Hair

Marketing Design,

Dallas, Texas

DESIGNER/

ILLUSTRATOR: Tom Hair

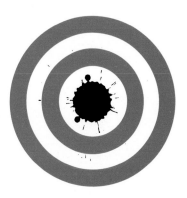

Peters Dental Associates

2508 Bay Area Blvd., Suite 100
Houston, Texas 77058
713/486-8061

Personalized Dental Care
for the Entire Family

DESIGN FIRM: Piland, Goodell & Pirnie, Inc., Houston, Texas
ART DIRECTORS: Don Goodell, Mike Borosky
DESIGNER: Mike Borosky
ILLUSTRATOR: David Piland

Peters Dental Associates

Valerie Malone
Dental Assistant

Peters Dental Associates
2508 Bay Area Blvd., Suite 100
Houston, Texas 77058
713/486-8061

Personalized Dental Care
for the Entire Family

A B C D E L I Z A B E T H I J K L
M N O P Q R S M I T H I J K L M N
O P Q R S T U V W X Y Z
C O P Y W R I T E R

2303 Spring Creek Lane
Atlanta, Georgia 30350
404 391·0777

Elizabeth Smith (Copywriter)

A B C D E L I Z A B E T H I J K L
M N O P Q R S M I T H I J K L M N
O P Q R S T U V W X Y Z
C O P Y W R I T E R

2303 Spring Creek Lane
Atlanta, Georgia 30350

DESIGN FIRM: Jane Hill

Design, Atlanta, Georgia

DESIGNER: Jane Hill

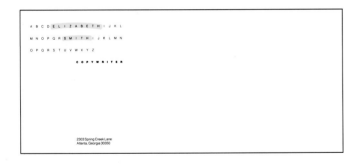

A B C D E L I Z A B E T H I J K L

M N O P Q R S M I T H I J K L M N

O P Q R S T U V W X Y Z

C O P Y W R I T E R

4 0 4 · 3 9 1 · 0 7 7 7

DESIGN FIRM: Grand Pré

& Whaley, St. Paul,

Minnesota

DESIGNER: Kevin

Whaley

Janet Virnig (Artists Representative)

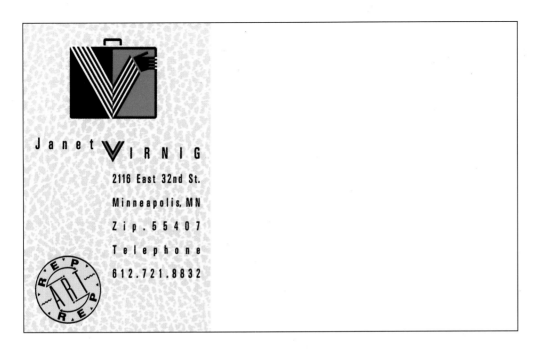

Janet **V**IRNIG

2116 East 32nd St.

Minneapolis, MN

Zip.55407

Telephone

612.721.8832

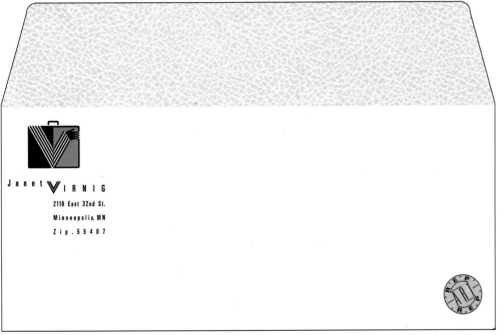

Janet **V**IRNIG

2116 East 32nd St.

Minneapolis, MN

Zip.55407

DESIGN FIRM:

Wondriska Associates,

Inc., Farmington,

Connecticut

ART DIRECTOR: William

Wondriska

DESIGNER: Christopher

Passehl

Mary Duffy Morris
Direct Marketing
Consultant and Writer
351 Pleasant Street Suite 122
Northampton MA 01060

Mary Duffy Morris
Direct Marketing
Consultant and Writer
413-584-7859
351 Pleasant Street Suite 122
Northampton MA 01060

Mary Duffy Morris
Direct Marketing
Consultant and Writer
413-584-7859
351 Pleasant Street Suite 122
Northampton MA 01060

Mary Duffy Morris (Direct Marketing Consultant & Writer)

John Rizzo Photography

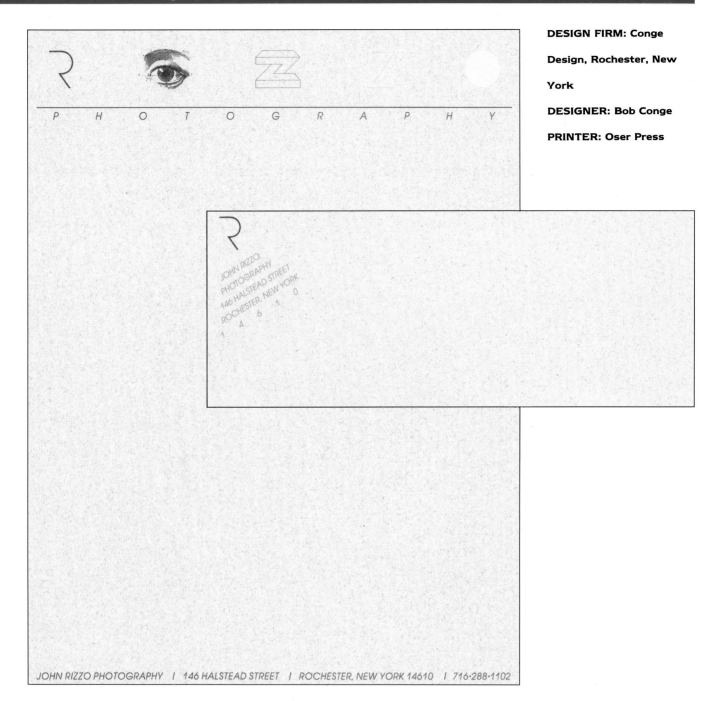

DESIGN FIRM: Conge Design, Rochester, New York

DESIGNER: Bob Conge

PRINTER: Oser Press

JOHN RIZZO PHOTOGRAPHY | 146 HALSTEAD STREET | ROCHESTER, NEW YORK 14610 | 716·288·1102

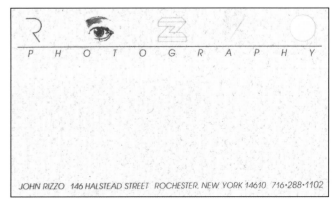

JOHN RIZZO 146 HALSTEAD STREET ROCHESTER, NEW YORK 14610 716·288·1102

STEPHANIE
SHIELDHOUSE
ILLUSTRATOR
2904 SOUTHERN AVE
BALTIMORE, MD 21214
301 254 7229

STEPHANIE
SHIELDHOUSE
ILLUSTRATOR
2904 SOUTHERN AVE
BALTIMORE, MD 21214

STEPHANIE
SHIELDHOUSE
ILLUSTRATOR
2904 SOUTHERN AVE
BALTIMORE, MD 21214
301 254 7229

DESIGNER/

ILLUSTRATOR: Stephanie

Shieldhouse, Baltimore,

Maryland

Stephanie Shieldhouse (Illustrator)

Warner Nurseries

37611 Pleasant Valley Road
Willoughby Hills, Ohio
44094

Telephone
216 946-0880

Warner Nurseries

37611 Pleasant Valley Road
Willoughby Hills, Ohio
44094

Telephone
216 946-0880

Warner Nurseries

37611 Pleasant Valley Road
Willoughby Hills, Ohio 44094

DESIGN FIRM: Kapp &

Associates, Cleveland,

Ohio

CREATIVE DIRECTOR:

Cathryn Kapp

DESIGNER: Tim Lachina

ILLUSTRATOR: Nan

Wiggins

THE COAST

1844 WEST

WAYZATA

BOULEVARD

LONG LAKE

MINNESOTA

5 5 3 5 6

612 476 2204

1844 WEST

WAYZATA

BOULEVARD

LONG LAKE

MINNESOTA

5 5 3 5 6

612 476 2204   TERRY ESAU

The Coast
MINNEAPOLIS·USA

The Coast
MINNEAPOLIS·USA

DESIGN FIRM: Mitchell Lindgren Type Design, Minneapolis, Minnesota
DESIGNER: Mitchell Lindgren

The Coast (Commercial Jingle Music)

THE COAST

1844 WEST

WAYZATA

BOULEVARD

LONG LAKE

MINNESOTA

5 5 3 5 6

DESIGN FIRM: Minnick

Advertising, Louisville,

Kentucky

DESIGNER: Norm

Minnick

HAYSLIP DESIGN ASSOCIATES

2602 McKinney Avenue

Suite 400

Dallas, Texas 75204

214/871-9106

343 West Manhattan Street

Santa Fe, New Mexico 87501

505/983-2147

HAYSLIP DESIGN ASSOCIATES

**DESIGN FIRM: Sullivan
Perkins, Dallas, Texas
ART DIRECTOR: Ron
Sullivan
DESIGNER: Linda Helton
ILLUSTRATOR: Willie
Baronet**

HAYSLIP DESIGN ASSOCIATES

2602 McKinney Avenue, Suite 400

Dallas, Texas 75204

214/871-9106

343 West Manhattan Street

Santa Fe, New Mexico 87501

505/983-2147

Debbie Walker Fain
Senior Designer

Hayslip Design Associates (Interior Design)

CLEAR LAKE
CHIROPRACTIC
ASSOCIATES

1020 BAY AREA BLVD., SUITE 106
HOUSTON, TEXAS 77058
(713) 486-7922

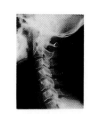

CLEAR LAKE
CHIROPRACTIC
ASSOCIATES

DR. HENRY D. NICOLAIDES
(713) 486-7922

1020 BAY AREA BLVD., SUITE 106
HOUSTON, TEXAS 77058

CLEAR LAKE
CHIROPRACTIC
ASSOCIATES

1020 BAY AREA BLVD., SUITE 106
HOUSTON, TEXAS 77058

DESIGN FIRM: Art City

Corporation, Houston,

Texas

DESIGNER: Jack Amuny

CLIENT: Dr. Henry

Nicolaides

Clear Lake Chiropractic Associates

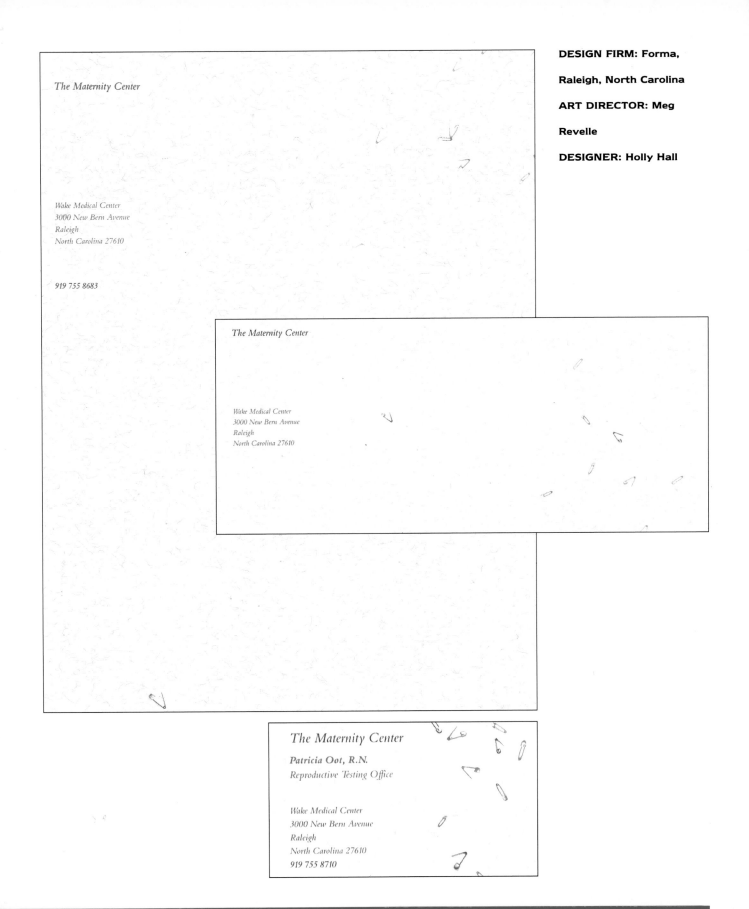

The Maternity Center

Wake Medical Center
3000 New Bern Avenue
Raleigh
North Carolina 27610

919 755 8683

The Maternity Center

Wake Medical Center
3000 New Bern Avenue
Raleigh
North Carolina 27610

The Maternity Center

Patricia Oot, R.N.
Reproductive Testing Office

Wake Medical Center
3000 New Bern Avenue
Raleigh
North Carolina 27610
919 755 8710

DESIGN FIRM: Forma,
Raleigh, North Carolina
ART DIRECTOR: Meg
Revelle
DESIGNER: Holly Hall

Maternity Center at Wake Medical Center

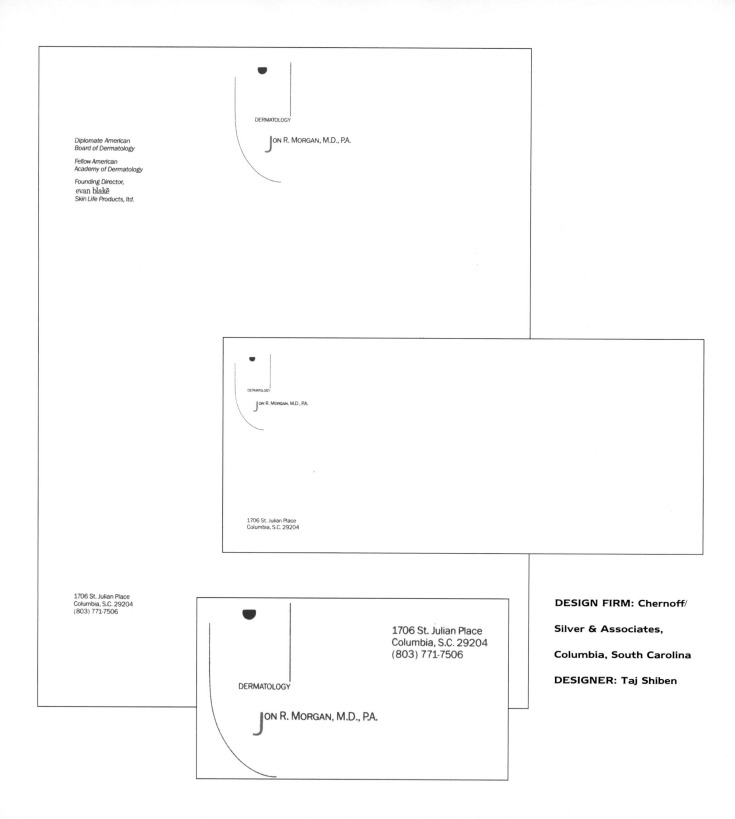

Diplomate American
Board of Dermatology

Fellow American
Academy of Dermatology

Founding Director,
evan blakē
Skin Life Products, ltd.

DERMATOLOGY

J ON R. MORGAN, M.D., P.A.

1706 St. Julian Place
Columbia, S.C. 29204

DERMATOLOGY

J ON R. MORGAN, M.D., P.A.

1706 St. Julian Place
Columbia, S.C. 29204
(803) 771-7506

1706 St. Julian Place
Columbia, S.C. 29204
(803) 771-7506

DERMATOLOGY

J ON R. MORGAN, M.D., P.A.

DESIGN FIRM: Chernoff/

Silver & Associates,

Columbia, South Carolina

DESIGNER: Taj Shiben

Jon Morgan (Dermatologist)

Judy Mills, Ms.T. • Certified Massage Therapist

P.O. Box 86594
San Diego, CA 92138

For Appointment:
619.226.5190

DESIGN FIRM: Bennett

Peji Design, La Jolla,

California

DESIGNER: Bennett Peji

Judy Mills, Ms.T. • Certified Massage Therapist

P.O. Box 86594
San Diego, CA 92138

Judy Mills, Ms.T. • Certified Massage Therapist

P.O. Box 86594
San Diego, CA 92138

For Appointment:
619.226.5190

KAREN RUBIN PHOTOGRAPHY
FOR CHILDREN OF ALL AGES
7144 EAST OHIO DRIVE
DENVER, COLORADO 80224
303·329·8173

KAREN RUBIN PHOTOGRAPHY
FOR CHILDREN OF ALL AGES
7144 EAST OHIO DRIVE
DENVER, COLORADO 80224
303·329·8173

KAREN RUBIN PHOTOGRAPHY
FOR CHILDREN OF ALL AGES
7144 EAST OHIO DRIVE
DENVER, COLORADO 80224
303·329·8173

DESIGN FIRM: DeOlivera
Creative, Inc., Denver,
Colorado
ART DIRECTOR: Richard
DeOlivera
DESIGNERS: Richard
DeOlivera, Chuck Trout
ILLUSTRATOR: Chuck
Trout

Karen Rubin Photography

A shop selling flowers, antiques, and contemporary objets d'art.
DESIGN FIRM: Gardner Greteman Mikulecky, Wichita, Kansas
DESIGNER: Sonia Greteman

ARTS À LA CARTE
2929 East Central
Wichita, Kansas 67214
316 652-0073

CLIENTS

Advertising Professionals of Des Moines **54**
Akers, Kevin **90**
Alamo Heights Pet Clinic **124**
Alejandro, Carlos **88**
Alford, Vivian **13**
Alfstad Blank Group, The **60**
Always There Dental Care **10**
Amigo, Marcial **77**
Amos, Wally **41**
Art Department, The **34**
Austin Nature Center **149**
Bel-Hop Studio **66**
Bender, Wesley James, Photography **36**
Black Dog Land Co. **144**
Bogdanovich, Greg **134**
Boshara, G.M., Inc. **91**
Brenner-Katz, Lauren, Advertising **40**
Brew Tech **45**
Bright Lights **102**
Bucha, Carolyn **29**
Bustamante, Gerald **13**
Butler, David, Illustration **49**
Camp Beverly Hills **32**
Carlson Ritchie, Leslie **18**
Chance, Dean, Creative **110**
Chargo Printing **34**
Chicago Dog and Deli **64**
Children's AIDS Network **72**
Children's Doctors, The **8**
Children's Museum of Atlanta **53**
City Lights **145**
Clear Lake Chiropractic Associates **168**
Coast, The **164**
Cooper Ladd, Carol **125**
Corporate Communications **142**
Covington, Neverne K. **100**
Dandy Candy Man, The **118**
Davidé Fur **98**
Departure Films **148**
Dog-Eared Businesses & Stuff **21**
Duffy Morris, Mary **160**
Dykes, John S. **14**
Earthly Pleasures **117**
Easterday Construction and Design **69**
Factory Limited, The **56**
Fagan, Mel, Swing Co. **12**
Farm to Market **76**

Farmworker Power Project **85**
Food Company, The **58**
Galleria Fair **173**
Garnand, David R. **73**
Graphic Gofers **136**
Greacen, Charles, Illustration & Graphics **94**
Greening, Helen, & Associates **135**
Grill Joss, Susan, Graphic Design/Illustration **140**
Grove, Bob, Design & Illustration **130**
Hair, Tom, Marketing Design **155**
Hantel, Johanna B. **52**
Harrington, Richard, Illustration **152**
Hayslip Design Associates **167**
Healthfast **42**
Hixenbaugh, Denise **116**
HōM **33**
House of Games **117**
IBM **96**
Imbrogno Photography **62**
Insite Architects **138**
Johnson Productions **99**
Kansas City Spine Center **112**
Kneapler, John, Design **117**
Kowalski, Stephen, Designworks **114**
Lake Street Shirts **128**
Lehman Graphic Design **86**
Lightman Plus Associates **106**
Little Designs **132**
Maclean Eckert Communications **37**
Maternity Center at Wake Medical Center **169**
McClear, Patricia **90**
Midland Research **44**
Mills, Judy **171**
Minimal Space Techline Studio **19**
Morgan, Jon **170**
Morreal, John A. **25**
Morris, Burton **116**
NAG Design **139**
Napoles Design Group **82**
Nicolaides, Dr. Henry **168**
No Dogs Design **154**
Noble Interior Design **84**
Peters Dental Associates **156**
Philip's Total Care Salon **80**
Pick's Multi-Restaurant Housing Systems **24**
Pitt, Stēv **22**
Popkin, Cameron D., Business Management **70**
Puder, Richard, Design **104**
Red Cap Building Services **119**
Redfern, Penny **122**
Rizzo, John, Photography **161**
Robin's Cookie Works **142**
Rubin, Karen, Photography **172**

Russ, Gary **108**
Sabin, Tracy, Illustration & Design **131**
Sanderson, James **92**
Schreibman Creative Services **120**
Scripts & Concepts, Inc. **146**
Seiniger Advertising **6**
Shamsey, Loretta **30**
Sharpe Illusions **111**
Shelby, L.C., Photography **166**
Shieldhouse, Stephanie **162**
Siebert, Terry Anne **143**
Smith, Elizabeth **157**
Spare Time Design **105**
Square Dogs Illustration **81**
St. Rita School for the Deaf **74**
Steinman, Nancy, Advertising Design **12**
Sunderland Smith Research Associates **28**
Suzanne's Cakes & Pastries **59**
Talcott, Julia, Illustration **116**
Taylor, James, & Associates **48**
Team Design **150**
Technical Publications **31**
Trousdell Design, Inc. **126**
Twigs, Inc. **26**
Typing to Go **65**
Urban, Pat **38**
Van Horn Photography **16**
Virnig, Janet **158**
Warner Nurseries **163**
Washington Mutual U.S. Track Cycling Championships 1989 **50**
Weeks, Marcy L. **95**
Wok 'n' Roll **78**
Work Rehabilitation Center (Texas Back Institute) **123**
Worley Construction Management **68**
Zimmerman, RC, and Associates **46**

DESIGN FIRMS

Alfstad Blank Group, The **60**
Armstrong Image Group **111**
Art City Corp. **168**
Arts & Letters Ltd. **148**
Beatson Vermeer Design **41**
Behr, Brenda, Advertising Design **18**
Behr-Lemons **135**
Bertz, Ted, Design, Inc. **59**
Blik, Tyler, Design **68**
Borders, Perrin & Norrander **12**
Brenner-Katz, Lauren, Advertising **40**
Caesar Studio **42**
Carr, Michael, Design **10**
Chernoff/Silver & Associates **170**
Conge Design **161**
Cooper Wingard Design **136**
Corporate Communications **142**
Crolick, Sue, Advertising & Design **128**
Davis Design **85**
DeOlivera Creative, Inc. **172**
Design Team One, Inc. **74**
Designed Marketing **148**
DeVault, Katherine, Design **120**
Dix & Eaton **142**
Dunlavey Studio, The **45**
Dunn and Rice Design **38**
Eisenberg, Pannell, St. George **24, 123**
Ely, Dorit, Design **143**
Evans/Spangler Design **50**
Forma **169**
Ganz Goldman **30**
Gardner Greteman Mikulecky **173**
Graffito, Inc. **58**
Grand Pré and Whaley, Ltd. **34, 158**
Greacen, Charles, Illustration & Graphics **94**
Griff, Ilene, Design **66**
Grill Joss, Susan, Graphic Design/Illustration **140**

Hair, Tom, Marketing Design **155**
Harrington, Richard, Illustration **152**
Held & Diedrich Design **78**
Hershey Associates **16**
Hill, Jane, Design **157**
Johnson, Dean, Design **69**
Kapp & Associates **163**
King, Rick, Design **48**
Kirsch, Art, Graphic Design **73**
Klassen Graphic Designs **149**
Kneapler, John, Design **117**
Knoth & Meads **44**
Kowalski, Stephen, Designworks **114**
Kuhn & Wittenborn **112**
Lawton, Bradford, Design Group, The **76**
Lehman Graphic Design **86**
Lewin Design Associates **26**
Lindgren, Mitchell, Type Design **164**
Linschoten & Associates Inc. **28**
Lipetz Design **125**
Little Designs **132**
Lofgreen, Art, Design **91**
Lopez Salpeter & Associates **96**
Louey/Rubino Design Group **98**
Maclean Eckert Communications **37**
Maris, West & Baker **90**
McClear Studios **90**
McKinlay and Partners **21**
Mekjavich, Elizabeth, Graphic Design **110**
Miller, Scott W., Design Group **6**
Miller, Victoria, Design **32**
Minnick Advertising **166**
Morreal Graphic Design **25**
Morris, Burton, Illustration **116**
NAG Design **139**
Napoles Design Group **82**
Nautilus Design **95**
No Dogs Design **154**
Obata, Kiku, & Co. **117**
Peji, Bennett, Design **171**
Penguin Studio/Press **65**
Pentagram Design **102**
Ph.D. **70**
Piland, Goodell & Pirnie, Inc. **156**
plus design inc. **80**
Pressley Jacobs Design Inc. **62**
Puder, Richard, Design **104**
Pushpin Group, The **72**
Ramsden Design **8**

RCR & Co. **108**
Rickabaugh Graphics **146**
River City Studio **49**
Runnion Design **119**
Sabin, Tracy, Illustration & Design **131**
Sayles Graphic Design **54, 64**
Shepherd, Robin, Studios **144**
Skolos/Wedell, Inc. **33**
Smidt, Sam, Inc. **19**
Smith, Larry, & Associates **84**
Smithgroup Inc. **106**
Spare Time Design **105**
Square Dogs Illustration **81**
Stanard, Michael, Inc. **36**
Steinman, Nancy, Advertising Design **12**
Stonecreek Designs **29**
Studio Bustamante **13**
Sullivan Perkins **167**
Talcott, Julia, Illustration **116**
Taylor/Christian Advertising, Inc. **99, 124, 138**
Team Design **150**
Tharp Did It **118**
Tippit Woolworth Design **117**
Toto Images **56**
Tracy, Jan, Design **22**
Trousdell Design, Inc. **53, 126**
Turk, Angela, Art & Copy **134**
Weeks & Associates **20**
Wiley Design **92**
Wondriska Associates, Inc. **160**

ART DIRECTORS DESIGNERS

Akers, Kevin **90**
Alford, Neva **139**
Alfstad, Sam **60**
Amigo, Marcial **77**
Amuny, Jack **168**
Anderson, Brent **24**
Armstrong, Tom **111**
Ayers, Catherine J. **65**
Beaton, Keri **59**
Behr, Brenda **18, 135**
Belichick, Patricia **31**
Benson, Chuck **142**
Bertz, Ted **59**
Bittman, Dan **74**
Blank, Peter J. **60**
Blik, Tyler **68**
Bollwerk, Teresa **117**
Borosky, Mike **156**
Brenner, Darrin **40**
Bruscato, Janet **150**
Bucha, Carolyn **29**
Bustamante, Gerald **13**
Butler, David **49**
Caesar, Delane **42**
Carr, Michael **10**
Chance, Dean **110**
Chavez, Marcos **36**
Christian, Roger **124**
Chwast, Seymour **72**
Coats, Todd **105**
Conge, Bob **161**
Cooper Wingard, JoAnne **136**
Covington, Neverne K. **100**
Crolick, Sue **128**
Cunninghame-Blank, Deborah **111**
Davis, Monique **85**
Dean, Bruce **69**
Dennis, Craig **145**
DeOlivera, Richard **172**
DeVault, Katherine **120**
Dunlavey, Michael **45**
Dunn, John **38**
Dykes, John S. **14**
Eckert, Lisa **37**
Eder, Susan **145**
Eisenberg, Arthur **24**
Ely, Dorit **143**
English, Claire **149**
Frederick, Anita **68**
Frederickson, Gregg **107**
Friedman, Bobbie **30**
Gant, Tim **78**
Goodell, Dan **156**

Gourley Lehman, Karen **86**
Grabarczyk, Lee **104**
Griff, Ilene **66**
Grill Joss, Susan **140**
Grove, Bob **130**
Hair, Tom **155**
Hall, Holly **169**
Hansen-Lynch, Ingrid **88**
Hantel, Johanna B. **52**
Harrington, Richard **152**
Helton, Linda **167**
Hershey, R. Christine **16**
Hill, Jane **157**
Hill, Lee A. **21**
Hill, Lisa **100**
Hodgson, Michael **70**
Hogin, Ross **50**
Huang, Jeffrey **56**
Ingebretsen, Elizabeth **92**
Jareaux, Robin **154**
Johnson, William Lee **62**
Kapp, Cathryn **163**
King, Rick **48**
Kirsch, Art **73**
Klassen, Alison **149**
Kneapler, John **117**
Kowalski, Stephen **114**
Kraft, Karyn **82**
Krumel, Mark **146**
Lachina, Tim **163**
Laney, Jody **76**
Lawton, Brad **76**
Lewin, Cheryl **26**
Lindgren, Mitchell **164**
Linschoten, Bud **28**
Lipetz, Jan **125**
Little, Judy **132**
Lofgreen, Art **91**
Louey, Robert **98**
Lun, Andy **56**
Martino, David **21**
McClear, Patricia **90**
McNeil, Nick **16**
Mekjavich, Elizabeth **110**
Meyer, Anita **80**
Miller, Scott W. **6**
Miller, Victoria **32**
Minnick, Norm **166**
Moran, Tim **148**
Morreal, Mary Lou **25**
Morris, Burton **116**
Napoles, Veronica **82**
Obata, Kiku **117**
Pannell, Cap **123**
Parisi, Joe **58**
Passehl, Christopher **160**
Peji, Bennett **171**
Peterson, Bryan **81**
Piercy, Clive **70**
Pirtle, Woody **102**
Puder, Richard **104**
Ramsden, Rosalie **8**
Redfern, Penny **122**
Remer, Arnold **46**
Revelle, Meg **169**

Richards, Paula 150
Rickabaugh, Eric 146
Riker, Curtis 108
Robinson, Randy 112
Rubino, Regina 98
Runnion, Jeff 119
Runnion, Sandy 119
Sabin, Tracy 131
Salpeter, Bob 96
Sayles, John 54, 64
Schifanella, Tom 144
Schweitzer, Dave 81
Serrano, José 44
Shepherd, Robin 144
Shiben, Taj 170
Shieldhouse, Stephanie 162
Short, Patrick 105
Sigman, David L. 142
Sizer, Patt 128
Skolos, Nancy 33
Smidt, Sam 19
Smith, Thom 106
Soto, Ken 68
Spangler, Kathryn 50
Steinman, Nancy 12
Stiegler Lupton, Karen 13
Sullivan, Ron 167
Sylvester, Mark 33
Talcott, Julia 116
Tharp, Rick 118
Thompson, Athena 12
Thompson, Tim 58
Tippit Woolworth, Carol 117
Tomlinson, Heidi 45
Tracy, Jan 22
Trousdell, Don 53, 126
Trousdell, Tina 126
Trout, Chuck 172
Turk, Angela 134
Vermeer, Dale 41
Weeks, Dan 20
Wells, Peter 81
Whaley, Kevin 34, 158
Wilcox, Mark 128
Wiley, Jean 92
Wilkens, Bill 95
Wilson, Mark 99
Wineman, Robin 84
Wondriska, William 160
Wynne-Jones, Bruce 123

ILLUSTRATORS
PHOTOGRAPHERS
COPYWRITERS
CALLIGRAPHERS
TYPOGRAPHERS
PRINTERS

Agnihotra Press, Inc. 136
Akers, Kevin 90
Alford, Vivian 13
Amigo, Marcial 77
Amos, Wally 41
Anderson, Brent 24
Barnhart, Mike 144
Barnhill, Steve 8
Baronet, Willie 167
Beaton, Keri 59
Blair Graphics 70
Bustamante, Gerald 13
Callahan, Murray 66
Campoverde, Raul 10
Carlson Ritchie, Leslie 18
Carr, Michael 10
Chance, Dean 110
Chwast, Seymour 72
Coats, Todd 105
Cooper Wingard, JoAnne 136
Cooper, Bob 144
Covington, Neverne K. 100
Cunninghame-Blank,
Deborah 110
Dean, Bruce 69
Deforest Printing 37
Dennis, Craig 145
DeVault, Jim 120
Dudak, Joe 64
Dykes, John S. 14
English, Claire 149
Espo Litho Inc. 86
Fineman, Michael 122
Francis, John 88
Friedman, Bobbie 30
Gaddis, Sara 74
Gale, Bill 135
Gant, Tim 78
Ganz, Bonnie 30
Garrett, Dan 41
Greacen, Charles 94
Great Faces 128
Grindeland, Bob 150
Grove, Bob 130
GS Printing 77
Guitteau, Jud 125
Hair, Tom 155
Hantel, Johanna B. 52
Harrington, Richard 152
Harris, Christine 41
Horn, Robert 37
House Graphics 25
Hudson, Karen 124
Johnson, Nancy 128

Juen, Nicole 80
Kantz, Bill 8
Kirsch, Charlotte 73
Kneapler, Charles 117
Krumel, Mark 146
Louey, Robert 98
Maclean, Deborah 37
McElhaney, Gary 108
Mills, Sue 18
Moran, Tim 148
Morris, Burton 116
Musgrave, Steve 62
Nelson, Bill 139
Ortega, Tony 85
Oser Press 161
Parisi, Joe 58
Peterson, Bryan 81
Piland, David 156
Post, George 114
Reppel, Aletha 42
Runnion, Jeff 119
Sabin, Tracy 44, 131
Sayles, John 64
Schweitzer, Dave 81
Shieldhouse, Stephanie 162
Siebert, Terry Anne 143
Sprankle, Rich 10
Talcott, Julia 116
Thompson, Athena 12
Tiani, Alex 96
Tomlinson, Kim 118
Tracy, Jan 22
Trout, Chuck 172
Typelink 25
Walima, Brian 110
Wells, Peter 81
Whaley, Kevin 34
Wiggins, Nan 163
Wilcox, Mark 138
Wilson, Mark 99
Wynne-Jones, Bruce 123
Yasui, Meredith 50
Yoshiyama, Glenn 50